CITY OF LIGHT

a play by
Anthony Clarvoe

based on the novel by
Lauren Belfer

BROADWAY PLAY PUBLISHING INC
New York
www.broadwayplaypublishing.com
info@broadwayplaypublishing.com

CITY OF LIGHT
© Copyright 2000, 2001 Anthony Clarvoe

Cover art: The Spirit of Niagara by Evelyn Rumsey Cary (1855-1924)

First edition: July 2023
I S B N: 978-0-88145-925-8

Book design: Marie Donovan
Page make-up: Adobe InDesign
Typeface: Palatino

In adapting *City of Light* for the stage, playwright Anthony Clarvoe has brilliantly transformed my novel into a dynamic theater piece. With edge-of-your-seat suspense, he explores the intimate emotional struggles of individuals while simultaneously illuminating the compelling and still-relevant social and political conflicts of America in 1901.

When I first saw Clarvoe's adaptation performed at the Studio Arena Theatre in Buffalo, New York, I was overcome by its nuanced intensity. And from that moment, the astonishing Kate Heasley Clarvoe became Louisa Barrett in my mind. She always will be.

I feel unending gratitude to everyone involved in the original production, especially Gavin Cameron-Webb, the Studio Arena's remarkable Artistic Director, who generously included me in discussions about each aspect of the project.

And I remain forever grateful to Anthony Clarvoe, for the profoundly moving gift of this play.

Lauren Belfer (2023)

CITY OF LIGHT was originally commissioned and developed by Studio Arena Theatre (Gavin Cameron-Webb, Artistic Director; Ken Neufeld, Executive Director).

The world premiere of CITY OF LIGHT was presented by Studio Arena Theatre, Buffalo, New York, on 11 September 2001. The cast and creative contributors were:

LOUISA BARRETT....................................Katherine Heasley
FRANCESCA COATSWORTH, MARIA LOVE ... Carolyn Swift
JOHN J ALBRIGHT, JAMES FITZHUGH,
BILLY..Richard Wesp
FREDERICK KRAKAUER, PRESIDENTS
CLEVELAND, ROOSEVELT, MCKINLEY .... Erick Devine
MARGARET SINCLAIR, SUSANNAH RILEY .... Angela Pierce
JOHN MILBURN, KARL SPEYER, ROLF.........Robert Rutland
FRANKLIN FISKE, PETER FRONCZYK,
RICHARD WATSON GILDER.............................Paul Todaro
PROFESSOR BARRETT, DEXTER RUMSEY,
DANIEL HENRY BATES..Lee Moore
YOUNG LOUISA, GRACE SINCLAIR ....Brianna Larson,
                                                                      Hillary Maloney
THOMAS SINCLAIR...................................Michael Chaban
MARY TALBERT .... Emily Yancey
POLICEMEN, SERVANTS, SPECTATORS, TERRORISTS, *etc.*
            Fernando Betancourt III, Carlton Franklin,
            James Fuetterer, Kelly Gregory, Dena Harrison

Director...Gavin Cameron-Webb
Scenic Designer .... William Barclay

Costume Designer .... Mariann Verheyen
Lighting Designer .... Phil Monat
Sound Designer .... Tom Mardikes
Original musical compositions .... Greg Mackender
Production Stage Manager .... Jessica Berlin
Dialect Coach .... Josephine Hogan
Assistant to the Director .... Jillian Pytlewski
Casting .... Elissa Meyers, CSA; Paul Fouquet, CSA

NOTES

This play was the reason we weren't in New York City on September 11, 2001.

The show was scheduled to open that night in Buffalo, New York. Many of the artists made our homes in Manhattan and Brooklyn. Having spent the morning watching, again and again, the coverage of the attack on the World Trade Center, calling and being called by friends and family to learn who was safe and who was missing, some of us were hesitant to present a play that featured political violence and an explosive act of terrorism. The management of Studio Arena Theatre never wavered: of course the show would go on. We wondered if anyone would come.

That night the audience filled every seat. They continued to do so for the rest of an extended run. In this time of trauma, which in a sense we have never left, people felt the need to gather in community and see a story about another time in our history when our country was in crisis.

A generation later, I am struck by the many ways Lauren Belfer's novel, in discovering parallels between the United States of that time and that of a century before, has proved prescient. Sexual abuses by powerful men and the seemingly total immunity granted to privilege, the struggle between industrialism and environmentalism, the demands for justice by African Americans and immigrants, the use of cultural philanthropy to whitewash corporate crimes, the fight of women to gain and keep the roles their talents deserve, our fears for our children, all this and more are here, and, alas, more topical than ever.

In Louisa Barrett, Lauren wrote a glorious, complicated heroine; the play turned her into a marathon role; and Katherine Heasley Clarvoe made from her a virtuosic performance. My thanks to them and to Gavin Cameron-Webb, who directed a spectacular production with clarity and grace.

Anthony Clarvoe

CHARACTERS & SETTING

(In order of actor appearance; grouped characters are played by the same actor)

LOUISA BARRETT, *headmistress, mid-30s*

FRANCESCA COATSWORTH, *architect,* LOUISA'*s friend, 40*
MARIA LOVE, *philanthropist, on* LOUISA'*s school board, 60*

JOHN J ALBRIGHT, *steel magnate, on* LOUISA'*s board, 53*
JAMES FITZHUGH, *engineer, 40s*
BILLY, *electrical worker, 40s*

FREDERICK KRAKAUER, *J P Morgan's man in Buffalo, late 40s*
GROVER CLEVELAND, *former president, a memory, 54*
THEODORE ROOSEVELT, *future president, 43*
WILLIAM MCKINLEY, *current president, 58*

MARGARET SINCLAIR, LOUISA'*s best friend, a ghost, mid-30s*
SUSANNAH RILEY, *art teacher at* LOUISA'*s school, 20s*

JOHN MILBURN, *lawyer, on* LOUISA's *board, 40s*
KARL SPEYER, *engineer, 40s*
ROLF, *electrical worker, 40s*

FRANKLIN FISKE, *reporter, 30s*
PETER FRONCZYK, *electrical worker, late 20s*
RICHARD WATSON GILDER, *writer, 40s*

PROFESSOR BARRETT, LOUISA's *father, a memory, 60s*
DEXTER RUMSEY, *millionaire, chair of* LOUISA's *board, 74*
DANIEL HENRY BATES, *nature preservationist, 60s*

YOUNG LOUISA, *a memory, 9*
GRACE SINCLAIR, LOUISA's *goddaughter, 9*

THOMAS SINCLAIR, *head of Niagara Frontier Power Project,*
Margaret's widower, GRACE's *adoptive father, 40*

MARY TALBERT, *wealthy African-American activist, 35*

POLICEMEN, SERVANTS, SPECTATORS, TERRORISTS, *etc.*

Buffalo, New York, 1901 & 1891; the Berkshires, 1901

ACT ONE

Scene 1:
Louisa Barrett's

(LOUISA BARRETT *lights a gas lamp. She remains for a moment, deep in thought.*)

(FRANCESCA COATSWORTH *enters the light, carrying sherry.*)

FRANCESCA COATSWORTH: They'd do anything for you. You know that, don't you?

LOUISA BARRETT: I know.

FRANCESCA COATSWORTH: We all would. I'd give up everything, take you around the world. Just say the word, *poof!* we'll be gone.

LOUISA BARRETT: I could never leave Buffalo.

FRANCESCA COATSWORTH: Oh, don't say it, don't think it! I'll take you to Asia! Angkor Wat. We'll mount an expedition into the jungle. How many elephants do you think we'll need?

LOUISA BARRETT: You're such a romantic.

FRANCESCA COATSWORTH: We'll have separate elephants, if you like. No? Because I hear after a long ride on a fast elephant, a lady is ready for anything. Oh, you're such a tease.

LOUISA BARRETT: I am nothing of the sort.

FRANCESCA COATSWORTH: I should just throw you down on the rug and have my way with you.

LOUISA BARRETT: Francesca.

FRANCESCA COATSWORTH: Yes, I know, but do you want to grow old alone? I would think you'd be grateful for some companionship. Passion.

LOUISA BARRETT: I would be grateful. Of course I would.

FRANCESCA COATSWORTH: Then you've certainly fooled everybody all these years.

LOUISA BARRETT: Yes. I suppose I have.

(JOHN J ALBRIGHT *enters, trailed by* FREDERICK KRAKAUER.)

JOHN J ALBRIGHT: Miss Barrett! I promised you a new face tonight.

LOUISA BARRETT: So you did, come in, Mr Albright.

JOHN J ALBRIGHT: Frederick Krakauer, Louisa Barrett.

FREDERICK KRAKAUER: Delighted.

LOUISA BARRETT: What brings you to Buffalo, Mr Krakauer?

JOHN J ALBRIGHT: Mr Krakauer is Mr J P Morgan's man.

(Beat)

LOUISA BARRETT: My goodness.

FREDERICK KRAKAUER: That's right. Looking after Mr Morgan's interests here.

LOUISA BARRETT: What are his interests?

FREDERICK KRAKAUER: Mr J P Morgan has more interests than you or I could dream of. Keeps track of everything, though. That's where I come in.

FRANCESCA COATSWORTH: Have some sherry, Mr Krakauer.

LOUISA BARRETT: May I present my very dear friend Francesca Coatsworth.

(MARGARET SINCLAIR *enters, very pregnant. No one acknowledges her except* LOUISA.)

FREDERICK KRAKAUER: Coatsworth. Now are you related to, ah—

FRANCESCA COATSWORTH: Yes, oh God, I'm related to everybody.

MARGARET SINCLAIR: *(Sitting, exhausted)* We all are.

JOHN J ALBRIGHT: If we didn't import new blood like Miss Barrett here, we'd be as inbred as show dogs.

FREDERICK KRAKAUER: I have a wife and three daughters on Staten Island myself.

FRANCESCA COATSWORTH: Well, that sounds like fun.

LOUISA BARRETT: New blood? I came here, what, twelve years ago?

JOHN J ALBRIGHT: You see? You *came* here. How refreshing.

(JOHN MILBURN *enters.*)

JOHN MILBURN: Evening, everybody! Evening, Miss Barrett!

JOHN J ALBRIGHT: Look out, here comes Milburn.

JOHN MILBURN: Miss Coatsworth! Where is the famous sherry!

(LOUISA BARRETT *leans to* MARGARET SINCLAIR, *who is sitting quietly listening.*)

LOUISA BARRETT: Can I get you anything, Margaret?

MARGARET SINCLAIR: Not a thing.

(JOHN MILBURN *accepts his sherry and descends upon the room.*)

JOHN MILBURN: Now!

FRANCESCA COATSWORTH: He sees your fresh face, Mr Krakauer.

JOHN J ALBRIGHT: Five dollars says the first words will be:

JOHN MILBURN: Mr Krakauer! Come to hear about the Pan-American Exposition?

FRANCESCA COATSWORTH: Too slow, Mr Albright.

(*Laughter*)

JOHN MILBURN: What?

FRANCESCA COATSWORTH: Albright just wasted some money.

JOHN MILBURN: Somebody must have a painting for sale.

(*Laughter.* FRANKLIN FISKE *enters, nods in thanks for his glass of sherry, and listens.*)

JOHN J ALBRIGHT: We all know each other far too well, Mr Krakauer. No secrets here.

JOHN MILBURN: Except one! Because I have just found out! I have here a wire from the White House! Confirming that on September the sixth, 1901, President William McKinley will be our guest at the Pan-American Exposition! He will meet the public and! throw the switch to start Powerhouse Three of the Niagara Frontier Power Project!

ALL: Bravo! Bravo!

JOHN MILBURN: What a coup, eh? The President! What a coup it will be!

JOHN J ALBRIGHT: Oh, I hope not a coup, John. We do want him still to be president when he leaves.

(Laughter)

JOHN MILBURN: Well, if there is, Vice President
Roosevelt's coming too!

(Laughter and applause)

FRANKLIN FISKE: So this is what prosperity sounds like.
Remarkable. I had no idea it had a sound.

JOHN MILBURN: Oh, it has many sounds, young man.
The symphony of progress, performed by the City of
Buffalo! The roar of the forges at Albright's steel mill.
The thunder of the generators at Niagara. The oohs and
ahhs of the public at the Pan-American Exposition—

JOHN J ALBRIGHT: And the relentless tub-thumping
boosterism of John Milburn! The Exposition hasn't
even opened yet, don't count your chickens.

JOHN MILBURN: I can dream, can't I?

LOUISA BARRETT: Of course you can, Mr Milburn.
That is the sound of prosperity. The sound of dreams
coming true. *(To* FRANKLIN FISKE, *on behalf of the room)*
We haven't met, Mister—

FRANKLIN FISKE: Forgive me, I should have introduced
myself. Franklin Fiske, arrived this week from New
York City. My cousin Susan is married to Mr Dexter
Rumsey of this city?

(There is a general lunge toward the great name.)

LOUISA BARRETT: Susan Fiske Rumsey, yes, of course.

JOHN MILBURN: How do you do, Mr Fiske.

JOHN J ALBRIGHT: Mr Fiske.

FRANCESCA COATSWORTH: So good to meet you.

(Even FREDERICK KRAKAUER *nods politely.)*

FRANKLIN FISKE: Yes, I hear that in Buffalo, if you know
a Rumsey, you know enough. Miss Barrett, your salon
deserves its glowing reputation.

(Amid the handshaking:)

JOHN MILBURN: *(To* LOUISA BARRETT*)* I thought we'd see Tom Sinclair this evening. He'll be thrilled about McKinley.

LOUISA BARRETT: Mr Sinclair is still in mourning.

JOHN MILBURN: Oh dear, of course he is.

MARGARET SINCLAIR: *(Quiet)* For me. Louisa? Tom's in mourning for *me*.

LOUISA BARRETT: God, you're right. You were dead by this time.

MARGARET SINCLAIR: Yes.

LOUISA BARRETT: I'm so sorry, Margaret. I was still thinking about you all the time.

*(*MARGARET SINCLAIR *exits.)*

FRANKLIN FISKE: Miss Barrett?

LOUISA BARRETT: Mm? *(With a start)* Mm. *(With a smile)* And what brings you to Buffalo, Mr Fiske?

FRANKLIN FISKE: Well, among other things, I hear you've got some kind of waterfall up here.

FRANCESCA COATSWORTH: *(A moan)* The Falls.

FRANKLIN FISKE: They must be a constant source of delight.

FRANCESCA COATSWORTH: *(Calling)* All right, when is the last time anyone went to the Falls?

JOHN J ALBRIGHT: The last time I had visitors from out of town.

(A general "mm hm" of agreement)

LOUISA BARRETT: There you have it, Mr Fiske. No appreciation for landscape.

FRANKLIN FISKE: I'm mostly interested in the power stations, myself.

JOHN MILBURN: As are we all.

JOHN J ALBRIGHT: He said interested in, not invested in.

FRANKLIN FISKE: My latest pursuit—latest of shamefully many, cousin Susan will tell you—is art photography.

JOHN MILBURN: Really! If you're looking for subjects for portraits, *I* could use a—

FRANKLIN FISKE: Actually, the portraits I take are of machines.

JOHN J ALBRIGHT: Close enough.

FRANKLIN FISKE: Factories, that sort of thing.

LOUISA BARRETT: Fascinating. Art should celebrate the industries that are transforming our lives.

FRANKLIN FISKE: And do you go to the Falls, Miss Barrett?

LOUISA BARRETT: No. Well. Only once.

JOHN MILBURN: Is that right?

LOUISA BARRETT: When I was a girl. Once was enough.

(In the near distance, the roar of Niagara. PROFESSOR BARRETT *enters, trailed by* YOUNG LOUISA, *both dressed for field work.)*

FRANKLIN FISKE: Sounds like a story.

LOUISA BARRETT: Not really.

PROFESSOR BARRETT: Feel how smooth the ledge is, Louisa? That's because the rocks have been under the water.

LOUISA BARRETT: We were at one of the Three Sisters Islands. Celinda Eliza, I think.

FRANCESCA COATSWORTH: We?

PROFESSOR BARRETT: The flow polishes them as slippery as glass.

LOUISA BARRETT: My father was a geologist at Williams College. In the summers, I tagged along on all his expeditions.

JOHN MILBURN: Really?

JOHN J ALBRIGHT: She said expeditions, Milburn, not Expositions.

PROFESSOR BARRETT: What we are hunting for now is glacial erratics. Boulders carried here by tidal waves of ice, some of them from hundreds of miles away.

YOUNG LOUISA: The pebbles are pretty. May I stay here?

PROFESSOR BARRETT: Try to stay dry.

(PROFESSOR BARRETT *wanders away, engrossed.* YOUNG LOUISA *crouches and peers into the water.*)

LOUISA BARRETT: He'd married late, my mother died when I was young, he didn't really know what to do with a little girl. He usually just thought of me as a very short undergraduate. That's what I thought, anyway.

YOUNG LOUISA: (*Seeing something in the water*) Papa! Papa, look! A diamond!

LOUISA BARRETT: A diamond. I was sure of it. There among the pebbles I saw a diamond.

JOHN J ALBRIGHT: I never saw you as a fortune-hunter, Miss Barrett.

LOUISA BARRETT: Once was enough, Mr Albright. It was bright and it shimmered. I had to have it, for my father. But the water kept carrying it further out into the stream. So I followed it. Further and further.

(YOUNG LOUISA *takes several slow steps forward.*)

PROFESSOR BARRETT: Louisa! Stop!

(PROFESSOR BARRETT *runs to* YOUNG LOUISA, *grabs her arm, pulls her back, and kneels before her.*)

PROFESSOR BARRETT: *(Shouting)* Don't you ever do that again! That was a stupid, stupid thing to do! Don't you know how strong the current is? You could have been swept over the Falls in an instant!

(PROFESSOR BARRETT *is crying. She is stunned. He holds her and leads her off, past* LOUISA BARRETT.)

(*One by one, quietly, the salon exits, too. The roar of the Falls fades away.*)

LOUISA BARRETT: And you'd think that would have taught me not to risk getting in over my head, wouldn't you? Ever again. You would think.

SUSANNAH RILEY: Miss Barrett? *(She comes into the light.)* I'm sorry, but I didn't know what to do. It was strange.

LOUISA BARRETT: What was strange, Miss Riley? Come in, warm up.

SUSANNAH RILEY: We were walking home, and—

LOUISA BARRETT: We?

SUSANNAH RILEY: Myself, some of the lower school girls. It was their day to volunteer with the poor children at the Crèche—

LOUISA BARRETT: And something happened.

SUSANNAH RILEY: Yes. Oh, no one bothered us, Miss Barrett, nothing like that. But one of the girls, she said…I thought you should know right away.

LOUISA BARRETT: Tell me what she said.

SUSANNAH RILEY: She said she wanted to kill herself. She said it like it was the most natural thing.

LOUISA BARRETT: Which girl was this?

SUSANNAH RILEY: Grace. Grace Sinclair. *(Beat)* She'd just been drawing for the kindergarteners, drawing elephants, they looked so real. She's very talented.

LOUISA BARRETT: Yes, I know.

SUSANNAH RILEY: Most of the poor children had never even seen a picture of an elephant. Then she imitated an elephant roaring—she's a fine mimic, Grace.

LOUISA BARRETT: Yes. And then when she threatened to kill herself...?

SUSANNAH RILEY: I tried to think of what you would say.

LOUISA BARRETT: Thank you, Miss Riley, what did you say?

SUSANNAH RILEY: I said—we were walking down Chapin Parkway and the lamps were coming on—and I said, how beautiful it was to see the lamplight on the snow—I said everything was so beautiful in the world. Was that the right thing to say, Miss Barrett?

LOUISA BARRETT: That was fine. What did *she* say?

SUSANNAH RILEY: Grace said everything *was* beautiful, but she was a bad girl. She said, "I want to be dead, so I won't be bad anymore." She was so quiet. I said, your mother would be sad if she could hear you talking like this and Grace said no, because when I'm dead I'll be with her in heaven, and I'll tell her I'm sorry, and that's why I'm going to kill myself.

LOUISA BARRETT: And then?

SUSANNAH RILEY: And then she made a snowball and threw it against a tree. Do you think she meant it, Miss Barrett?

LOUISA BARRETT: Of course not. *(Clapping her hands lightly)* You won't discuss this.

SUSANNAH RILEY: No, Miss Barrett.

LOUISA BARRETT: It will be our secret.

(SUSANNAH RILEY *exits*. LOUISA BARRETT *remains.*)

Scene 2:
Sinclairs'

(GRACE SINCLAIR *runs in.*)

GRACE SINCLAIR: Aunt Louisa!

LOUISA BARRETT: Good afternoon, Grace.

GRACE SINCLAIR: *(In an Irish accent)* Will you be wanting some tea, ma'am?

(Off LOUISA BARRETT's *look, in her own voice:)*

GRACE SINCLAIR: Mrs Sheehan and the others are out. At a *wake*. Have you ever been to a wake?

LOUISA BARRETT: A wake? No.

GRACE SINCLAIR: I think it's like your birthday party, but you're dead.

LOUISA BARRETT: Where is your father?

THOMAS SINCLAIR: *(As he enters; an Irish accent)* A bit behind, as usual. Forgive me, Louisa. And speaking of a bit behind, I wouldn't want somebody's headmistress to know the fearful state of somebody's homework—

GRACE SINCLAIR: It's practically done.

THOMAS SINCLAIR: I know your practically dones, miss. My new generator is practically done, and it wouldn't put the glow in a light bulb. When you're actually done, come join us again.

(GRACE SINCLAIR *exits.*)

LOUISA BARRETT: You got my note?

THOMAS SINCLAIR: Yes, about Grace.

LOUISA BARRETT: How has she seemed to you lately?

THOMAS SINCLAIR: Why, is there a problem at school?

LOUISA BARRETT: Have you seen any change in her?

THOMAS SINCLAIR: Has she done something, what?

LOUISA BARRETT: No. Why do you ask?

THOMAS SINCLAIR: Do you find… Have *you* noticed anything? I have started to see things, things that don't seem like herself, gestures. I've thought she might have got them from those other people.

LOUISA BARRETT: What other people?

THOMAS SINCLAIR: Her real parents. When she was a newborn, I wondered what the father looked like, and the mother, and then it didn't matter, she was ours, but now…It's like she's taking after somebody else. She used to be so much like Margaret.

LOUISA BARRETT: She may just be getting to be herself. She's growing up.

THOMAS SINCLAIR: You've been away from us too long.

LOUISA BARRETT: I thought perhaps, without Margaret…

THOMAS SINCLAIR: You were *our* friend, Louisa. And Grace's godmother, you're still the only one who knows the truth about her being adopted. Still our secret.

LOUISA BARRETT: Yes.

THOMAS SINCLAIR: Evening's coming on. (*Crossing to the wall*) I've been waiting for someone to show this to.

(THOMAS SINCLAIR *turns a switch. The room is flooded with electric light.*)

LOUISA BARRETT: Oh!

THOMAS SINCLAIR: Well, I am turning water into light. I am doing that.

LOUISA BARRETT: When did you bring electricity into the house?

THOMAS SINCLAIR: It was one of the first things I did, after Margaret died.

LOUISA BARRETT: It's striking, Tom. Look at you. Plain as day.

THOMAS SINCLAIR: Most people don't realize. They see the streetlamps and the railway, the steel mill going up at Stony Point, but…Electricity is changing the nature of life itself.

LOUISA BARRETT: Even the air feels different.

THOMAS SINCLAIR: That it does, you're right! Electricity doesn't burn away the oxygen in the room, the way gaslight does. Someday I'm going to send hydroelectric power to every house in five states. Then the country. When the factories are electrified, machines will do the dangerous jobs, not men. Not boys like I was, working all night running cheap bottles from the benches to the ovens; a conveyer belt will do that. Boys will be home, learning to read—by electric lamps. They won't be afraid anymore.

LOUISA BARRETT: Afraid of what?

THOMAS SINCLAIR: Afraid of the dark. Weren't you ever afraid of the dark?

LOUISA BARRETT: I was raised by a scientist. It wasn't allowed.

(A knock on the door.)

THOMAS SINCLAIR: Odd, a visitor this time of night.

(GRACE SINCLAIR runs through toward the door.)

LOUISA BARRETT: Would you talk to my students sometime? About electricity?

THOMAS SINCLAIR: You believe electricity is a proper topic for young ladies?

LOUISA BARRETT: Anything is a proper topic for young ladies, when presented in the proper manner. By the proper person.

THOMAS SINCLAIR: Well now.

LOUISA BARRETT: Would you? It would mean a great deal to Grace.

THOMAS SINCLAIR: Oh, I doubt that Grace wants to hear any more about electricity.

(GRACE SINCLAIR *enters with* KARL SPEYER.)

GRACE SINCLAIR: *(Irish)* Excuse me, sir, ma'am. A Mister Karl Speyer to see the master.

THOMAS SINCLAIR: Mr Speyer! Good evening!

KARL SPEYER: Mr Sinclair.

THOMAS SINCLAIR: Excuse me, Louisa, this is…an uncommon intrusion. Miss Louisa Barrett, Mr Karl Speyer. Mr Speyer is—

LOUISA BARRETT: The Westinghouse engineer.

KARL SPEYER: *(Kissing her hand)* Miss Barrett. You are a font of knowledge.

LOUISA BARRETT: That is my job description: experienced schoolmarm, font of knowledge. I read about you in the newspapers.

THOMAS SINCLAIR: No problems, I hope, to bring you here this evening? Come into the parlor.

(THOMAS SINCLAIR *and* KARL SPEYER *exit.*)

GRACE SINCLAIR: *(In her own voice)* I wonder why he came here.

LOUISA BARRETT: Business. Something to do with the power station.

GRACE SINCLAIR: But we're in mourning. No one is supposed to come here.

THOMAS SINCLAIR: *(Off)* Now that's absurd, Speyer!

KARL SPEYER: *(Off)* I will tell what you are doing!

THOMAS SINCLAIR: *(Off)* Don't you threaten me!

(GRACE SINCLAIR puts her hands over her ears.)

KARL SPEYER: *(Off)* I have done what you asked! When is enough?!

THOMAS SINCLAIR: *(Off)* God damn it, Speyer!

KARL SPEYER: *(Off)* When is enough?!

(A door slams. The voices continue indistinctly.)

GRACE SINCLAIR: Mama and Papa fought about electricity. Mama would cry.

LOUISA BARRETT: Grace, all people disagree sometimes. Even married people. It's one of the ways they come to understand each other.

GRACE SINCLAIR: My parents only had fights about electricity.

LOUISA BARRETT: Didn't Margaret want to electrify the house?

GRACE SINCLAIR: Mama thought Papa was trying to take too much water from Niagara Falls. "You won't be happy until we're picnicking on the precipice", that's what she said.

LOUISA BARRETT: Your mother was trying to make a point. She didn't mean that people would actually picnic on the riverbed at the Falls, that's absurd. No one could take that much water.

GRACE SINCLAIR: You don't know what made my mother die.

LOUISA BARRETT: Grace. I do know. I was here, remember? Your mother gave birth to her baby before the baby was ready, and the baby died, and your mother got sick from it. But she'd want us to be looking forward now, to the future.

GRACE SINCLAIR: I hate electricity!

LOUISA BARRETT: Electricity is our future. How can you hate electricity?

GRACE SINCLAIR: Joan of Arc didn't have electricity, Cleopatra didn't have electricity, Queen Elizabeth didn't have electricity. My mother didn't have electricity.

LOUISA BARRETT: Grace? Grace.

(KARL SPEYER *enters*, THOMAS SINCLAIR *following*. KARL SPEYER *nods quickly and exits.*)

LOUISA BARRETT: Is everything all right?

THOMAS SINCLAIR: Oh, Mr Speyer has a flair for the dramatic. Sorry you had to hear that. Best if we all put it out of our minds.

LOUISA BARRETT: I should go.

THOMAS SINCLAIR: Homework!

GRACE SINCLAIR: *(In her Irish accent again, subdued)* Good night, ma'am. *(She exits.)*

THOMAS SINCLAIR: Was there something else you wanted to tell me?

LOUISA BARRETT: No. That was all.

(THOMAS SINCLAIR *exits.* LOUISA BARRETT *watches him go. She remains.*)

Scene 3:
Delaware Park

(FRANKLIN FISKE *enters.* FREDERICK KRAKAUER *watches at a distance.*)

FRANKLIN FISKE: Did you know him?

LOUISA BARRETT: I beg your pardon?

FRANKLIN FISKE: The deceased.

LOUISA BARRETT: The…

(POLICEMEN *cross, carrying a stretcher.*)

FRANKLIN FISKE: They'll be fishing him out of there soon, Miss Barrett, you may not want to stay.

LOUISA BARRETT: Drowned…

FRANKLIN FISKE: We've met, at your salon the other night, I don't know if you—

LOUISA BARRETT: Mr Fiske, yes, of course I remember.

FRANKLIN FISKE: Did you know him?

LOUISA BARRETT: Who?

FRANKLIN FISKE: The deceased. Karl Speyer.

LOUISA BARRETT: Karl Sp… Not exactly.

FRANKLIN FISKE: That's an unusual response.

LOUISA BARRETT: Why are you asking the question?

FRANKLIN FISKE: Point taken. Old habits die hard. The journalistic boys down there were speculating about the death.

LOUISA BARRETT: You spoke with them?

FRANKLIN FISKE: I used to be one of them, long ago. The New York *World*'s man in the Philippines. I have an appointment with the deceased. But he seems to be standing me up. I was going to photograph a new electrical generator of which he was unduly proud.

Thomas Sinclair—you know who he is, don't you? Director of the electrical project?

LOUISA BARRETT: Why.

FRANKLIN FISKE: The boys talked with Sinclair this morning: he loved "poor Karl" like a brother, never a harsh word with him—

LOUISA BARRETT: Really?

FRANKLIN FISKE: "Really" what? Why does that surprise you?

LOUISA BARRETT: Well, because—doesn't one often have harsh words with one's brother? At least in childhood. Of course, I never had a brother.

FRANKLIN FISKE: Are you sure you didn't know Karl Speyer?

LOUISA BARRETT: Why are you sure that I did?

FRANKLIN FISKE: I find people seldom linger at a death site for no reason.

(*Two* POLICEMEN *cross carrying the stretcher, which holds a body under a tarp.*)

LOUISA BARRETT: You may know "people", Mr Fiske, but you do not know me. I am pursuing a study of the efficiency of the police department. I visit murder scenes totally out of civic concern.

FRANKLIN FISKE: Murder scenes? So you think this was a murder?

LOUISA BARRETT: No. I simply assumed, as the police would do, that it is a possibility.

FRANKLIN FISKE: A man falls through the ice and you assume it was murder. Buffalo must be even more exciting than I thought. Good luck with your inquiry, Miss Barrett.

LOUISA BARRETT: Good luck with yours, Mr Fiske.

FRANKLIN FISKE: Oh, I have no inquiry, Miss Barrett. I'm just a concerned citizen, like yourself.

(FRANKLIN FISKE *exits.* LOUISA BARRETT *watches the policemen while* MARIA LOVE, JOHN MILBURN, JOHN J ALBRIGHT, *and* DEXTER RUMSEY *enter and the scene changes to:)*

Scene 4:
The Buffalo Club

MARIA LOVE: Murder? That is absurd!

JOHN J ALBRIGHT: The more absurd the better, that's the yellow press for you.

JOHN MILBURN: Absurd—it's dangerous! Have you read them?

JOHN J ALBRIGHT: Read the newspapers? I'm a businessman, I have no time for historical fiction.

JOHN MILBURN: When they write about Speyer's death, they write about the power station and its investors! I did not make this investment to link my good name with the word murder!

MARIA LOVE: Let the coroner do his work, then we'll know.

JOHN MILBURN: Let's order the coroner to call it an accident, then we'd know for certain.

JOHN J ALBRIGHT: Thank God we have a lawyer on the board.

DEXTER RUMSEY: I spoke to Butler over at the *News*. *(In the silence)* He told me that as publisher he has no interest in the truth or falsity of a murder accusation. His only interest is in selling newspapers. I can hardly interfere with his pursuit of business. But. Today we have news of our own.

JOHN MILBURN: Indeed! Miss Barrett! However did you keep it to yourself?

LOUISA BARRETT: Keep what?

JOHN MILBURN: "Keep what?" she says. Still waters, Miss Barrett, still waters.

JOHN J ALBRIGHT: Babbling brooks, Milburn, babbling brooks.

MARIA LOVE: Miss Barrett has always been the soul of discretion.

LOUISA BARRETT: Thank you, Miss Love, but I am at a loss to know what I've been discreet about.

DEXTER RUMSEY: Forgive us, then, Miss Barrett. The Board has received word of a substantial donation to the Macaulay School.

MARIA LOVE: More than substantial. Shocking.

(Handing DEXTER RUMSEY a document:)

JOHN MILBURN: You might begin with this one, Mr Rumsey.

DEXTER RUMSEY: Thank you, Milburn. *(Reading)* "The Macaulay School is hereby awarded an endowment of one million dollars—"

LOUISA BARRETT: What?

DEXTER RUMSEY: "—the yearly income from which is to be used solely at the discretion of Miss Louisa Barrett, headmistress—"

MARIA LOVE: Absolutely irresponsible, encouraging the recipient of charity to spend it however she likes. Wanton extravagance the result.

LOUISA BARRETT: Who—who has—

DEXTER RUMSEY: "This endowment is made by Thomas Sinclair—"

LOUISA BARRETT: Wh— Why?

DEXTER RUMSEY: "—in honor of his beloved wife, the late Margaret Winspear Sinclair, class of 1886."

LOUISA BARRETT: A million dollars.

JOHN J ALBRIGHT: You seem surprised, Miss Barrett. Hadn't Mr Sinclair made you aware of his plans?

LOUISA BARRETT: I did not have an inkling, and I was just…

(Beat)

JOHN MILBURN: Remind me never to play poker with Thomas Sinclair.

JOHN J ALBRIGHT: Or else with Miss Barrett.

LOUISA BARRETT: Truly, Mr Albright—

DEXTER RUMSEY: We think it only proper to offer Sinclair a place on the board. An unusual step, given that he is somewhat—new to the city. Miss Barrett? Do you approve?

LOUISA BARRETT: Yes, yes, of course I approve.

DEXTER RUMSEY: If you have any objection…?

LOUISA BARRETT: Given that he is no newer to the city than I, I can scarcely object on those grounds.

DEXTER RUMSEY: My dear Miss Barrett. You are one of us. You know that.

JOHN J ALBRIGHT: What on earth will you do with all that money?

LOUISA BARRETT: Oh, I don't… A chemistry laboratory. Microscopes, a microscope at every desk. A telescope. A swimming pool, a running track—

JOHN J ALBRIGHT: Why not a whole new gymnasium?

MARIA LOVE: Hush! (She exits.)

LOUISA BARRETT: Why not! With basketball courts—my girls love basketball. I want Francesca Coatsworth to do the design.

DEXTER RUMSEY: Naturally you do.

LOUISA BARRETT: And scholarships! So many scholarships! Poor girls, smart ones, who never would have had the opportunity—

DEXTER RUMSEY: Steady on, Miss Barrett.

JOHN J ALBRIGHT: Try not to lower the tone of the place too much, will you?

JOHN MILBURN: Appropriate enough, given the source.

(Beat)

LOUISA BARRETT: Given the source, Mr Milburn?

JOHN MILBURN: Oh, good heavens, Miss Barrett, I don't mean you.

LOUISA BARRETT: I didn't think you did, Mr Milburn. I was merely thinking that it would be appropriate, scholarships, after all, where would Thomas Sinclair be today, if you, Mr Albright, had not sponsored his education? A new generation is reaping the benefit of your investment in him.

JOHN J ALBRIGHT: I can hardly argue with that, now, can I. Neatly done, Miss B.

DEXTER RUMSEY: Macaulay will be the preeminent school for girls in the country. With this funding, and this leadership.

LOUISA BARRETT: Forgive me. When I said I was new to the city, I only…I was an orphan when I came here. A penniless orphan. This city has given me…you have given me… *(She puts her hands to her face.)*

DEXTER RUMSEY: Well, my friends, here's something we shall keep among ourselves. Old Tom Sinclair has made our Miss Barrett cry.

(As the Board disperses:)

JOHN J ALBRIGHT: Miss Barrett, may I ask a favor?

LOUISA BARRETT: Of course.

JOHN J ALBRIGHT: I assume Tom Sinclair has told you something of his plans.

LOUISA BARRETT: For the school? As I told you—

JOHN J ALBRIGHT: *(After seeing that they are alone)* No. For the power station. What he's up to out there. Has he changed his plans, since Karl Speyer's death?

LOUISA BARRETT: I don't know.

JOHN J ALBRIGHT: Give Sinclair a message for me? Tell him that I have my finger in the dike, but I can't hold the waters back much longer. Apt phrase, don't you think? In the context?

LOUISA BARRETT: Why don't you tell him yourself?

JOHN J ALBRIGHT: I have, I have. But I hope that hearing my message from you will be more persuasive. You *are* young Grace Sinclair's godmother, after all. Good, good.

LOUISA BARRETT: I'm not sure I understand.

JOHN J ALBRIGHT: Then I'll give you some advice: deliver my message and ask Sinclair his plans. Once you know, never tell anyone and stay as far away from all of this as you can.

(JOHN J ALBRIGHT exits. LOUISA BARRETT remains.)

Scene 5:
Francesca Coatsworth's

(FRANCESCA COATSWORTH *and* MARY TALBERT *enter.*
FRANCESCA COATSWORTH *carries a roll of building plans.*)

FRANCESCA COATSWORTH: Louisa. We're just finishing
up—

LOUISA BARRETT: I'm sorry, am I—

FRANCESCA COATSWORTH: Mrs Talbert is about to
engage me to design a substantial renovation for her
home.

MARY TALBERT: We shall see, Miss Coatsworth.

FRANCESCA COATSWORTH: Mrs Mary Talbert, Miss
Louisa Barrett—

MARY TALBERT: Miss Barrett, I know your work.

LOUISA BARRETT: I am a great admirer of yours, Mrs
Talbert.

MARY TALBERT: I wish I had *your* admirers. A million
dollars.

LOUISA BARRETT: Yes. You've heard about that.

FRANCESCA COATSWORTH: Everybody's heard about
that.

MARY TALBERT: In all my years as an educator, in all
my years in the struggle, never did I hear of such a gift.

LOUISA BARRETT: Nor I. I can't imagine what would
cause a person to make such a great donation.

MARY TALBERT: The usual reasons: to please his public,
to ease his conscience, to appease his God. In that
order. It will mean great changes for your school.

LOUISA BARRETT: Yes, of course.

MARY TALBERT: And for yourself. You have been
granted a good deal of freedom, haven't you.

LOUISA BARRETT: Yes.

MARY TALBERT: And how do you plan to use your freedom, Miss Barrett?

LOUISA BARRETT: How do you mean?

MARY TALBERT: A question for another day. Miss Coatsworth, keep striving, I'm sure you'll get it right soon. I should like to call on you, Miss Barrett. I shall not cause you embarrassment by visiting during school hours.

LOUISA BARRETT: Mrs Talbert, you could never—

MARY TALBERT: You needn't pretend, you know what I mean.

LOUISA BARRETT: Of course.

MARY TALBERT: Good evening. *(She exits.)*

FRANCESCA COATSWORTH: I need a drink.

LOUISA BARRETT: God yes. Frannie? You're rich. Why do rich people give people money?

FRANCESCA COATSWORTH: Same as anybody. So they'll go to bed with us. *(Opening the plans)* Now let's see if I meet with someone's approval today.

LOUISA BARRETT: Frannie, this is striking.

FRANCESCA COATSWORTH: This elevation shows the new construction. Gothic Revival exterior, the turrets, eaves, and towers match the present school building... You're not even looking.

LOUISA BARRETT: I'm sorry, it's just...Frannie, why do you think Mr Sinclair gave the school all this money?

FRANCESCA COATSWORTH: It's made you the talk of the drawing rooms, you know.

LOUISA BARRETT: Talk. About me.

FRANCESCA COATSWORTH: Oh, it will be all right, it will probably—

LOUISA BARRETT: What are they saying?

FRANCESCA COATSWORTH: Some people are saying he wants a memorial to Margaret. Some people say it's an apology for Margaret.

LOUISA BARRETT: What about Margaret?

FRANCESCA COATSWORTH: Really, Louisa, you're so dense. People say that he—

LOUISA BARRETT: Oh, none of you can get over it, she could have had a man from any of your families and she chose an Irish Catholic from nothing.

FRANCESCA COATSWORTH: Margaret died trying to give that man another child.

LOUISA BARRETT: I saw her almost every day. She was happy.

FRANCESCA COATSWORTH: Most people think Sinclair's trying to buy something.

LOUISA BARRETT: Buy what? Most people buy their way onto the Macauley board so they can lunch with Mr Rumsey once a month. But it's too much money.

FRANCESCA COATSWORTH: Perhaps he wants to buy his daughter a better education.

LOUISA BARRETT: Perhaps. But a million dollars, that's absurd.

FRANCESCA COATSWORTH: Well, she is quite a handful.

LOUISA BARRETT: Why do you say that?

FRANCESCA COATSWORTH: I was visiting the Rumsey estate on Saturday, a birthday luncheon for one of my little cousins, I can't remember which. Grace Sinclair was there, as a guest of the birthday girl. Ruth Rumsey, that's right. Well, I went to hug little Ruthless hello,

and Grace was beside her, so I went to hug her too.
And Grace Sinclair went stiff as a board, and shouted,
"You're not my mother, get away from me, my
mother's dead and I wish I was too." I quite knew how
she felt.

LOUISA BARRETT: Oh, Frannie…

FRANCESCA COATSWORTH: She was pounding her leg
with her fist, it was… Then she ran outside and hid.

LOUISA BARRETT: Was she all right?

FRANCESCA COATSWORTH: Little Ruthless ran out to
find her, and five minutes later they were climbing
trees. *She* was fine. *(Beat)* Some people think Sinclair's
trying to create a diversion.

LOUISA BARRETT: From what, from Grace?

FRANCESCA COATSWORTH: From that man's death.

LOUISA BARRETT: Karl Speyer? Why would he need to
do that?

FRANCESCA COATSWORTH: "We're all fine! Still getting
rich out here! Nothing sneaky going on!" This could be
the biggest scandal in Buffalo since Grover Cleveland
left town.

LOUISA BARRETT: What do *you* think Mr Sinclair is
buying?

FRANCESCA COATSWORTH: Isn't it obvious? He's bought
you.

LOUISA BARRETT: Honestly.

FRANCESCA COATSWORTH: Honestly yourself. I saw
how he looked at you, even when Margaret was alive.

LOUISA BARRETT: There is nothing between me and
Thomas Sinclair.

FRANCESCA COATSWORTH: As far as the drawing rooms are concerned, you're his now. You're "That Miss Barrett who got a million dollars from Tom Sinclair."

LOUISA BARRETT: And here I thought they all thought you and I were...you know.

(Beat)

FRANCESCA COATSWORTH: I'm done being your cover, Louisa. If you've started something with Thomas Sinclair, I won't cover for you.

LOUISA BARRETT: What are you talking about?

FRANCESCA COATSWORTH: "My very good friend, Francesca Coatsworth"—I'm there to serve the sherry and reassure the wives that their husbands will be safe at your salon. It was fine as long as there was nothing else going on, a girl can dream, but if there is something—

LOUISA BARRETT: There is nothing going on, Frannie!

FRANCESCA COATSWORTH: If there were, would you know?

(A light knock)

FRANCESCA COATSWORTH: Anyway, I have another interest developing. A requited interest.

(SUSANNAH RILEY enters.)

SUSANNAH RILEY: Sorry—am I early? The young lady downstairs said to—

FRANCESCA COATSWORTH: You're right on time. Look who's here, Miss Riley.

SUSANNAH RILEY: Miss Barrett. Good evening.

LOUISA BARRETT: *(Examining the plans)* Good evening, Miss Riley. Miss Coatsworth and I were reviewing the plans for the addition to the school. I see you're going to have a beautiful new art studio.

SUSANNAH RILEY: Yes, I know. The entire addition is going to be beautiful.

LOUISA BARRETT: Ah. You've seen it already.

FRANCESCA COATSWORTH: Miss Riley has been so interested in everything I've shown her. Once she got over her scruples on the subject.

SUSANNAH RILEY: Miss Coatsworth—

FRANCESCA COATSWORTH: The subject of course being the source of the funds for her studio: Mr Thomas Sinclair, defiler of Niagara.

LOUISA BARRETT: Why don't I let you get on with your evening.

SUSANNAH RILEY: But Miss Barrett, don't you think— Thomas Sinclair is stealing the waters of Niagara to make—what? Electrified factories? To make aluminum? Grinding wheels? Is that what we want, to turn the beauty of Niagara into grinding wheels?

FRANCESCA COATSWORTH: And art studios, dear.

SUSANNAH RILEY: The art studio, the entire addition, that's just a kind of cover. So he can do what he wants and no one will object. It's a lie. It's immoral.

FRANCESCA COATSWORTH: Well.

LOUISA BARRETT: Why shouldn't the water do something useful? Who are you to say that aluminum and grinding wheels and silicon carbide and steel don't help humanity more than water falling over a cliff?

SUSANNAH RILEY: But Miss Barrett, they'll never stop, you know that.

LOUISA BARRETT: The Falls has too much water for its own good, anyway. The constant rock slides, the erosion. My father was a geologist, I have been studying this subject since I was a young girl—

SUSANNAH RILEY: But—they'll keep going until Niagara is bare rock, from the rapids to the gorge—

FRANCESCA COATSWORTH: There, there, we're just talking—

SUSANNAH RILEY: And the beauty, the irreplaceable beauty—as an artist, I can feel—

LOUISA BARRETT: As an artist.

FRANCESCA COATSWORTH: Oh God.

LOUISA BARRETT: As an artist you know things, yes, see things the rest of us can't, is that right?

SUSANNAH RILEY: Miss Barrett, I only—

LOUISA BARRETT: As artists, you all seem to believe that the truth consists in how you feel about things. But there are facts, Miss Riley, facts which are not always apparent to the untrained eye, however sensitive that eye may be to the pleasures of irreplaceable beauty. However entitled she may feel to her own exclusive use of it!

(SUSANNAH RILEY *runs out.* FRANCESCA COATSWORTH *looks at* LOUISA BARRETT *for a moment, and follows* SUSANNAH RILEY. LOUISA BARRETT *remains, as the lights change.)*

Scene 6:
Lincoln Parkway

(LOUISA BARRETT *turns to walk, but stops as three workmen enter, looking up.)*

ROLF: You see it?

PETER FRONCZYK: Maybe…no.

BILLY: What a neighborhood. Palaces.

ROLF: Makes a change. Is that it?

PETER FRONCZYK: I don't see it.

BILLY: *(Spotting* LOUISA BARRETT*)* Hey, I see that.

PETER FRONCZYK: Hey.

ROLF: If you like bluestockings.

BILLY: Hey, blue fire's the hottest, you know?

ROLF: Hey!

PETER FRONCZYK: Hey, I know you! Miss Barrett?

BILLY: Hey, no, I know you first!

PETER FRONCZYK: *(To the men)* Knock it off. *(To* LOUISA BARRETT*)* Miss Barrett. Sorry about—I'm Peter Fronczyk. My sister—

LOUISA BARRETT: Maddie Fronczyk. Senior class. Scholarship to Cornell.

PETER FRONCZYK: Talks about you all the time. Sorry about these guys.

LOUISA BARRETT: What are you all doing here?

PETER FRONCZYK: Oh, the power lines leading to Mr Sinclair's house. Somebody shorted them out again.

LOUISA BARRETT: Again?

PETER FRONCZYK: What's the name of that fancy boy's school?

LOUISA BARRETT: What? The Nichols School.

PETER FRONCZYK: They toss a wire over the lines, watch it pop. Think it's funny.

LOUISA BARRETT: That's terrible.

ROLF: You think it's boys? No, I think this here is a message from the union men. First Karl Speyer, next Mr Sinclair.

LOUISA BARRETT: Is that true, Peter? People think Mr Speyer was murdered?

ROLF: What about it, Pete?

PETER FRONCZYK: Shut up, you guys.

BILLY: No, Miss, Pete's just trying to make more work for us, ain't it, Pete?

PETER FRONCZYK: Yeah, that's right, it was me. How do you like the overtime you're getting?

ROLF: What is overtime?

BILLY: We're not getting any overtime.

PETER FRONCZYK: That's because we don't have a union.

ROLF: He's a smart boy.

BILLY: Good brain on that boy.

ROLF: Yeah, when J P Morgan sends the Pinkertons to shoot him boom in the head, we'll say, look at all those good brains Peter Fronczyk used to have.

PETER FRONCZYK: All right, fine, there's the short, let me get up that pole.

ROLF: Yeah, yeah.

PETER FRONCZYK: Give me the safety harness?

ROLF: What's a safety harness?

BILLY: We got no safety harness.

PETER FRONCZYK: That's because we don't have a union!

BILLY: Hey, shut up.

(THOMAS SINCLAIR *and* GRACE SINCLAIR *enter.*)

GRACE SINCLAIR: *(Running to* LOUISA BARRETT*)* Aunt Louisa! What are you doing here!

LOUISA BARRETT: I was coming to see you and your Papa.

THOMAS SINCLAIR: Good evening, Miss Barrett. Boys!

PETER FRONCZYK, BILLY & ROLF: Mr Sinclair, evening, sir.

THOMAS SINCLAIR: Rolf, Billy.

LOUISA BARRETT: Mr Sinclair. Someone has been attacking your house?

THOMAS SINCLAIR: Not exactly. How's it looking up there, boys?

ROLF: Right there, sir.

THOMAS SINCLAIR: Ah, yes.

LOUISA BARRETT: Who, do you think?

THOMAS SINCLAIR: Ah, who knows. Nobody very serious. Maybe the preservationists.

LOUISA BARRETT: You think so?

THOMAS SINCLAIR: Daniel Henry Bates, those people.

BILLY: In front of the power station every day, signs and shouting. Louder than the picket lines.

THOMAS SINCLAIR: Want to keep all God's light to themselves. Or it might be one of the unions. What do you think, Peter Fronczyk?

PETER FRONCZYK: Anything's possible.

THOMAS SINCLAIR: That it is, that it is. That's the spirit. These bold men here, Grace, are called hot stick men.

GRACE SINCLAIR: Why?

BILLY: Because if we put one hand wrong, little girl, that's what we'll be, a hot stick—

THOMAS SINCLAIR: Stow that, Billy.

BILLY: Yes, sir, sorry.

THOMAS SINCLAIR: I'm surprised to see you among 'em, Peter. Thought you had more upstairs.

PETER FRONCZYK: The money's better, Mr Sinclair.

THOMAS SINCLAIR: Carrying the family since your Da went?

PETER FRONCZYK: Since he had the accident, yes, sir.

THOMAS SINCLAIR: All this and fomenting revolution in my power station, must keep you busy, son. Isn't that so? I hear you're one of the best organizers the unions have got in there. Isn't that so, boys?

(Beat)

PETER FRONCZYK: Anything's possible, sir.

THOMAS SINCLAIR: That it is. That it is. But I don't think it'll be possible to keep you in this job. Just isn't safe.

(Beat)

GRACE SINCLAIR: Aunt Louisa, can we go?

LOUISA BARRETT: In a minute, sweetheart.

PETER FRONCZYK: Listen, Mr Sinclair—

THOMAS SINCLAIR: Now. As you'll be needing a job, I've got an opening for a board operator. Training position. Interested?

PETER FRONCZYK: That's a management job.

THOMAS SINCLAIR: 'Tis, yes. Smart young man shouldn't be climbing with his legs. Ought to be climbing with his brains. Well?

PETER FRONCZYK: Sir...

THOMAS SINCLAIR: Rolf. What would his Da have said?

ROLF: Well, sir.

BILLY: His Da would have said not to be a Goddamn fool.

GRACE SINCLAIR: Oh!

BILLY: Begging your pardons.

LOUISA BARRETT: Come with me, Grace.

GRACE SINCLAIR: In a minute.

THOMAS SINCLAIR: Billy's right, Peter. Well?

PETER FRONCZYK: Yes, sir. All right.

THOMAS SINCLAIR: Good lad. Rolf, you take the high post, would you? Grace, would you take Mr Fronczyk up to the kitchen, tell Mrs Sheehan to get something hot ready for the boys when they're done. That all right with you fellas?

BILLY & ROLF: Yes, sir, Mr Sinclair.

THOMAS SINCLAIR: Off you go, then.

ROLF: Good bye, Pete! (*He climbs up and out of sight.*)

BILLY: Don't forget us, Mr Fronczyk!

PETER FRONCZYK: Shut up.

(PETER FRONCZYK *and* GRACE SINCLAIR *exit.* BILLY *climbs up and out of sight.*)

LOUISA BARRETT: That was…

THOMAS SINCLAIR: Management. That was management.

LOUISA BARRETT: Well, it couldn't have gone better if you'd planned it.

THOMAS SINCLAIR: Know when to spot an opportunity.

LOUISA BARRETT: Speaking of which…

THOMAS SINCLAIR: I got your note. You're very kind.

LOUISA BARRETT: I don't know how to thank you.

THOMAS SINCLAIR: You already have. By the way, I turned down a position on your board of directors.

LOUISA BARRETT: Why?

THOMAS SINCLAIR: I feel no need to lunch with Dexter Rumsey once a month. Think you can manage all that money without me?

LOUISA BARRETT: Yes, of course.

THOMAS SINCLAIR: Good.

LOUISA BARRETT: Tom, I was coming to deliver a message. From John Albright.

THOMAS SINCLAIR: Interesting.

LOUISA BARRETT: He asked me if you'd changed your plans for the power station, since Karl Speyer's death.

THOMAS SINCLAIR: What did you say?

LOUISA BARRETT: I said I didn't know.

THOMAS SINCLAIR: Anything else?

LOUISA BARRETT: He said to tell you that he has his finger in the dike, but he can't hold out much longer.

(THOMAS SINCLAIR *laughs.*)

LOUISA BARRETT: What does it mean?

THOMAS SINCLAIR: It means old John hasn't lost his sense of humor.

LOUISA BARRETT: Can you tell me what you're doing?

THOMAS SINCLAIR: But I have.

(GRACE SINCLAIR *runs back on.*)

GRACE SINCLAIR: Papa, Aunt Louisa, come on!

(THOMAS SINCLAIR *and* GRACE SINCLAIR *exit. As* LOUISA BARRETT *is about to follow,* FREDERICK KRAKAUER *detaches himself from a shadow.*)

FREDERICK KRAKAUER: Miss Barrett.

LOUISA BARRETT: Mr Krakauer.

FREDERICK KRAKAUER: So you know Thomas Sinclair.

LOUISA BARRETT: His wife was my best friend. She died last year.

FREDERICK KRAKAUER: Yes, condolences. And you're godmother to his girl.

LOUISA BARRETT: Yes.

FREDERICK KRAKAUER: Quite a fella. Self-made man.

LOUISA BARRETT: Yes.

FREDERICK KRAKAUER: Knows that power station like nobody else. Anything happened to him, we'd be in big trouble. At least until the new station goes on line.

LOUISA BARRETT: Yes.

FREDERICK KRAKAUER: You think he remembers his factory days? Folks who knew him when? Compatriots, fellow workers…comrades?

LOUISA BARRETT: He was just a boy.

FREDERICK KRAKAUER: Think he keeps in touch?

LOUISA BARRETT: I wouldn't know.

(BILLY *climbs down and exits.*)

FREDERICK KRAKAUER: Funny we've never really spoken, you and I.

LOUISA BARRETT: Yes. I see you almost everywhere I go.

FREDERICK KRAKAUER: Not everywhere. Can't be everywhere. Wish I could.

LOUISA BARRETT: In public, at the homes of my friends…

FREDERICK KRAKAUER: Just looking after Mr J P Morgan's interests.

LOUISA BARRETT: Does that include Mr Sinclair's power station?

FREDERICK KRAKAUER: Is that what Mr Sinclair calls it? His power station?

LOUISA BARRETT: No. Not exactly. My words, not his.

FREDERICK KRAKAUER: Big operation there. Lots for
a new man to learn. Penstocks, turbines, generators.
Know who taught me the most? Poor old Karl Speyer.

LOUISA BARRETT: Poor man.

FREDERICK KRAKAUER: Yes.

LOUISA BARRETT: Some people say he was murdered.

FREDERICK KRAKAUER: I know. But it's a silly way to
kill somebody. Sure, you could hold a gun on a man,
make him walk across the ice, he comes to a weak spot,
he falls in. There's easier ways to kill a man.

LOUISA BARRETT: If someone wanted to make it look
like an accident, though.

FREDERICK KRAKAUER: With a man who goes to
Niagara Falls all the time? Accidents happen every
day up there. No, there's lots of easier ways. Unless…

LOUISA BARRETT: Unless?

FREDERICK KRAKAUER: Mr Morgan has a saying. A man
always has two reasons for what he does—a good one,
and the real one. Maybe whoever did it just wanted
to show people he could get to anybody, anytime,
anywhere. That could be worth the trouble.

LOUISA BARRETT: It's late, Mr Krakauer, and I have a
meeting, so—

FREDERICK KRAKAUER: Mighty late for a meeting.

LOUISA BARRETT: And I don't wish to be later. Excuse
me.

FREDERICK KRAKAUER: If you find anything out…

LOUISA BARRETT: I'll know where to find you.

FREDERICK KRAKAUER: No need. I'll be around. (He
exits.)

Scene 7:
Louisa Barrett's.

(LOUISA's office enters, along with MARY TALBERT.*)*

MARY TALBERT: Miss Barrett. It is good of you to see me so late.

LOUISA BARRETT: It was good of you to come to me.

MARY TALBERT: Your school is a handsome place.

LOUISA BARRETT: Do you miss your own teaching?

MARY TALBERT: I have never stopped teaching. I am organizing, working toward suffrage, fighting against lynching, providing vocational training. We are teachers, Miss Barrett. Everything we do is teaching.

LOUISA BARRETT: I know what you mean.

MARY TALBERT: Good. This endowment from Mister Sinclair. You're going to have a first-class school here.

LOUISA BARRETT: We have *always* striven to be the best school in the city of Buffalo. The girls should have no less than the boys. That has been a point of particular pride with me.

MARY TALBERT: I'm sure. Who is your city, Miss Barrett? Who is Buffalo?

(Beat)

LOUISA BARRETT: No, we do not have any colored students.

MARY TALBERT: Never have had any colored students.

LOUISA BARRETT: In that we are hardly unusual.

MARY TALBERT: No. I couldn't see the motto carved above the door here, is that what it says? "The Macaulay School: Hardly Unusual?" Is that who you are?

LOUISA BARRETT: We are a private school. The fees are
high.

MARY TALBERT: Prohibitively high.

LOUISA BARRETT: A part of those fees goes to fund a
few scholarships.

MARY TALBERT: And now you have the funds to
provide many more.

LOUISA BARRETT: And you want me to provide one to a
girl from your community?

MARY TALBERT: Absolutely not. I will not have it said
that the first colored girl to enter and to graduate from
the Macaulay School was here as a special case. No. I
have a niece, Millicent, a bright girl, bright as any of
your girls here.

LOUISA BARRETT: I'm sure.

MARY TALBERT: And the fees will not be a barrier to us.
Once Millicent shows these people, then the ones you
give the scholarships to can follow her, and they and
everyone will know it can be done. It can be done, Miss
Barrett. You said you admire my work? This is my
work, this right here. It can be your work, too.

LOUISA BARRETT: If it were up to me…

MARY TALBERT: Tell me who it's up to.

LOUISA BARRETT: There is my board, for a start.

MARY TALBERT: Your Mr Dexter Rumsey and my
husband are on the best of terms. They do business
together in real estate. Miss Maria Love and I serve on
several of the same committees. They know us. Really
it comes down to you.

LOUISA BARRETT: Not entirely.

MARY TALBERT: The parents? Surely they will follow
Mr Rumsey's lead.

LOUISA BARRETT: I will be candid. My students come from a very narrow sphere of privilege. They have never known any colored girls who were not household servants. Girls of this age are so sensitive to any difference at all. They assume any difference to be a sign of inferiority.

MARY TALBERT: You make your students sound… profoundly ignorant.

LOUISA BARRETT: I'm afraid, in this respect, they are.

MARY TALBERT: Well, you are their teacher, Miss Barrett. Educate. Educate.

LOUISA BARRETT: I try. My students volunteer one afternoon a week with the poor children at the Crèche—

MARY TALBERT: The poor immigrant children. One day there will be a school in our community, as good as Macaulay. In the meantime, we cannot lose Millicent's whole generation. I would be…grateful, for what you can offer.

LOUISA BARRETT: Mrs Talbert, I sympathize, truly I do, but—

MARY TALBERT: I appreciate your sympathy, but it will not suffice. You are a public figure, Miss Barrett, like it or not.

LOUISA BARRETT: My school will not take sides in public disputes.

MARY TALBERT: The laws turn more and more against us, and still we try to work within them. Meanwhile, whoever killed that Karl Speyer has shaken the powers that be to their roots. There are people in my community who may take the same kind of action to achieve such results. If my way is to prevail, I must show some results.

LOUISA BARRETT: Is that a threat?

MARY TALBERT: It is a fact.

LOUISA BARRETT: I have a school to run. I do what I can, behind the scenes.

MARY TALBERT: This is a game to you, isn't it? A game of wheedling and dealing in the secrecy of your salon. But the time is coming when the secrets will be revealed. When people will have to stand up and say who they are and what they stand for.

(MARY TALBERT exits as:)

Scene 8:
Lyric Hall

(Lights up on DANIEL HENRY BATES, standing at a lectern.)

DANIEL HENRY BATES: Good evening. My name is Daniel Henry Bates.

(A crowd forms itself into an audience. LOUISA BARRETT joins the people entering and finding seats: FRANCESCA COATSWORTH, FRANKLIN FISKE, FREDERICK KRAKAUER, JOHN MILBURN. SUSANNAH RILEY is on the platform close to DANIEL HENRY BATES.)

DANIEL HENRY BATES: What are we talking about, when we talk about Niagara? It is transcendence. Sublimity. The divine. Yes, when we talk about Niagara, we talk about the Lord God. Nature is a manifestation of the divine. The contemplation of nature leads us to the divine. And so when we stare into the green waters of Niagara, we are staring into the face of God. What is it that the power company wishes to do with this manifestation of God? They intend to turn it into bits of steel and aluminum and electric light. Ask yourself this, my friends: who owns the Falls of Niagara? Is it J. Pierpont Morgan and your own Thomas Sinclair and John Albright and Dexter P Rumsey? Or is it the lovers of nature and God?

FRANCESCA COATSWORTH: Beautiful.

LOUISA BARRETT: He is well spoken.

FRANCESCA COATSWORTH: Not him. Susannah, she's like one of those saints hearing voices. Ecstasy.

LOUISA BARRETT: Standing up there...

(JAMES FITZHUGH *hurries onto the platform and quickly shuffles through his notes.*)

JAMES FITZHUGH: Sorry, sorry, sorry... First of all, I wish to—oh, I'm James Fitzhugh, Acting Chief Engineer of the Niagara Frontier Power Project, and I know you were expecting Karl Speyer, who was the Chief Engineer of the Niagara Frontier Power Project, but he is unable, of course, to be here this evening, being...dead, so I'm here, James Fitzhugh, Acting Chief Engineer, speaking for the entire staff and directors of the Niagara Frontier Power Project, to say we share Mr Bates's concerns. The preservation of an adequate scenic effect at Niagara has always been foremost in our minds. The Falls at Niagara are a source of daily amazement and spiritual comfort to us all.

FRANCESCA COATSWORTH: Gray little man. Couldn't they do any better?

LOUISA BARRETT: He's a scientist, Francesca. With facts.

FRANCESCA COATSWORTH: Like I said. Oo, here comes Jehovah again.

DANIEL HENRY BATES: They tell us they'll only take a teeny, weeny, insy, binsy bit of water. But we know them, don't we? We know they won't be happy until not one drop of water flows across Niagara's precipice. Already, the American Falls are shrinking. Soon they will be nonexistent. Dry rock from the shore to Goat

Island. Then the broad Horseshoe Falls will begin to
shrink, narrower and narrower and narrower and so
to nothing. Lake Erie itself will become unnavigable.
The water level will sink—even in the great harbor of
Buffalo ships will run aground.

JAMES FITZHUGH: In fact, our work is saving Niagara.
As many of you know, the Falls suffers a natural
recession of as much as four feet per annum or more.
The cataract is destroying itself. In the thousands of
years since its creation, the cataract has cut a gorge
some seven miles long, from the Queenston Bluff
to its present location. By lessening the water's
incessant grinding at the limestone and shale of the
escarpment, we significantly slow this natural process
of destruction.

DANIEL HENRY BATES: More than ten million gallons
a minute, they're taking now. Isn't it enough? Over a
foot off the depth, they're taking now. Isn't it enough?

JAMES FITZHUGH: Mr Bates's diversion figure would
equal thirty-six thousand cubic feet per second, which
is absurd. The maximum capacity of a powerhouse is
no more than nine thousand cubic feet per second...

FRANCESCA COATSWORTH: (A moan) Oh God.

JAMES FITZHUGH: ...Now as we can see, the power
station diverts seven million gallons a minute,
(Continuing under the following) which equals no more
than three to six inches off the depth at any given time.
Such usage is minuscule within the overall context, and
completely unnoticeable. The depth at the center of the
Horseshoe Falls is estimated at approximately twenty
feet—

FRANKLIN FISKE: (Over JAMES FITZHUGH) Wait. He's
trying to slip something past us, telling us the usage for
one powerhouse, when they have, what, two on-line,
another one coming?

FRANCESCA COATSWORTH: *(Over* JAMES FITZHUGH*)* Oo. Sneaky little bastard.

LOUISA BARRETT: *(Over* JAMES FITZHUGH*)* It's like a mix of facts and something else, why is he…I hate that. What is he hiding?

*(*DANIEL HENRY BATES *and* JAMES FITZHUGH *begin interrupting and talking over each other:)*

DANIEL HENRY BATES: They will try to trick us! They will tell us electricity is good for us, that it brings us wonderful things—

JAMES FITZHUGH: Thanks to hydroelectric power, Niagara does give benefits to all of us, not just sightseers like Mr Bates—

DANIEL HENRY BATES: No one but the rich will ever have electric lights!

JAMES FITZHUGH: It reduces our dependence on coal, and the labor unrest that disrupts the coal industry—

DANIEL HENRY BATES: Gaslight makes for glorious streetlamps!

JAMES FITZHUGH: It replaces coal, the air becomes cleaner—

DANIEL HENRY BATES: Horsepower has willingly pulled our trolleys for generations!

JOHN MILBURN: *(Calling from the audience)* I wonder if he asked the horses about that!

JAMES FITZHUGH: —creates thousands of jobs throughout the area. *(Shouting)* And Niagara is not "gone!" Our charters from the state of New York would never permit us to take all the water. Water use is strictly controlled and subject to frequent inspections.

DANIEL HENRY BATES: Inspections. Inspections. *(Brandishing a piece of paper)* I have here a list—a list of

New York State water inspectors being bribed to look
the other way while the power station steals God's
water. I will not humiliate the men on this list by
reading it aloud. Not yet.

FRANKLIN FISKE: So, you think there's anything written
on that paper?

(JOHN MILBURN *makes his way to the platform.*)

JAMES FITZHUGH: Well, I want to say first of all in
response to that, that...

JOHN MILBURN: May I interject a word here? May
I? John Milburn. Evening, everybody. With all due
respect for the speakers thus far, I wish to enter this
debate from a somewhat different angle. I'm a God-
fearing man. I worship my God each week at Trinity
Church, as many of us do.

FRANCESCA COATSWORTH: Appeal to crass elitism, not
bad.

JOHN MILBURN: "And God said, Let us make man
in our image, after our likeness: and let them have
dominion...over all the earth." In the sight of God, men
are more important than waterfalls. God has given the
great Falls at Niagara to man, to do with what he will,
for the benefit of mankind. Well, is there any greater
benefit than the easing of back-breaking labor? Than
the lighting of the darkness? We are making light at
Niagara. Is not light the symbol of God incarnate? And
if light is the symbol of God incarnate, then electricity
is a manifestation of the divine. God's plan for Niagara
and His plan for Buffalo are one and the same. When
the work at Niagara is complete, we will be the greatest
city in America. Let us embrace our future—and
permit our future to embrace us.

(*Applause and hubbub as the crowd breaks up and exits and
the lights change.*)

Scene 9:
Outside Lyric Hall

(LOUISA BARRETT *and* FRANKLIN FISKE *remain.*)

FRANKLIN FISKE: I haven't seen a hijacking that neat since the South China Sea. John Milburn is on the board of the power station, isn't he?

LOUISA BARRETT: I believe so.

FRANKLIN FISKE: And on the board of your school?

LOUISA BARRETT: How well you've come to know our community, Mr Fiske, in so very short a time.

FRANKLIN FISKE: I like to know where I am. Don't you? (*Beat*) A million dollars.

LOUISA BARRETT: Yes, Mr Fiske.

FRANKLIN FISKE: Nice round figure, easy to pronounce. Congratulations.

LOUISA BARRETT: Thank you.

FRANKLIN FISKE: Were you expecting this gift before the evening you spent in Sinclair's home? The evening Karl Speyer died?

LOUISA BARRETT: What makes you say I was visiting the Sinclairs that night?

FRANKLIN FISKE: Sinclair's alibi was that he was at home with his daughter and her godmother. I asked cousin Susan, "Who is Grace Sinclair's godmother?" Well, surprise! She's you! Who was at the park lake the day after Speyer's death, studying the crime scene out of a sense of civic duty? You again! And who just got a million-dollar windfall from Thomas Sinclair? Well, how do you do again! What happened while you were at his house?

LOUISA BARRETT: What is your stake in this, Mr Fiske? What is your concern with my goddaughter and me?

FRANKLIN FISKE: Perhaps I wish to be your protector.

(LOUISA BARRETT *laughs bitterly.*)

FRANKLIN FISKE: I mean it. From the moment I saw you by the lake, I can't get you out of my mind.

LOUISA BARRETT: Mr Fiske. No more compliments. They always imply a desire for something. As do offers of protection. Let us confine ourselves to facts.

FRANKLIN FISKE: What makes you think I want something?

LOUISA BARRETT: You have not given up journalism to become a gentleman picture-taker. Your eye is too sharp and your nose is too keen. The New York *World* has a long tradition of undercover reporting. What are you here to investigate?

(*Beat*)

FRANKLIN FISKE: The power station at Niagara Falls. Irregularities there.

LOUISA BARRETT: There is nothing "irregular" about the power station.

FRANKLIN FISKE: You're right, it's going the way these things usually do. Karl Speyer wanted to show me the new generator he'd named for himself: the Westinghouse-Speyer. He claimed it made more electricity with less water.

LOUISA BARRETT: I've read about it.

FRANKLIN FISKE: Speyer was concerned about the overuse of water. Had a healthy skepticism about the goals of his bosses. Or an unhealthy skepticism. The man has been murdered. I want to know why and by whom. Don't you?

LOUISA BARRETT: If that were true, of course I would.

FRANKLIN FISKE: That day at the murder site, I told you Sinclair said he and Speyer had never had a harsh word, and you said, "Really?" You were surprised. Why?

LOUISA BARRETT: *(Fumbling with her reticule)* No reason. As I told you at the time—

FRANKLIN FISKE: No reason? Honestly—

LOUISA BARRETT: I'm sorry if that angers you, Mr Fiske.

FRANKLIN FISKE: Why shouldn't I be angry? I've got the sharpest mind in this benighted city working against me.

LOUISA BARRETT: Who is that?

FRANKLIN FISKE: Why, you, Miss Barrett. *(Pointing at her hand)* What is that?

LOUISA BARRETT: No more compliments, Mr Fiske.

FRANKLIN FISKE: Not compliments. Facts. *(Pointing at her hand)* What on earth is that?

LOUISA BARRETT: This is change, Mr Fiske, for the streetcar, which I am about to board. Have you any further questions?

FRANKLIN FISKE: Not that. That.

LOUISA BARRETT: What?

(FRANKLIN FISKE reaches into her hand, plucks something out, and holds it up: an old campaign button.)

LOUISA BARRETT: Mr Fiske! What on earth!

FRANKLIN FISKE: "Reelect Grover Cleveland"?

LOUISA BARRETT: Mr Fiske, this is outrageous!

FRANKLIN FISKE: It certainly is! Grover Cleveland?!

LOUISA BARRETT: Give that back!

FRANKLIN FISKE: Grover Cleveland?! How long has he been in your reticule?

LOUISA BARRETT: You are the nosiest person I have met in my life!

FRANKLIN FISKE: It is an unexpected fact, Miss Barrett, I had to pick it up. I shall have to ask cousin Susan about this.

LOUISA BARRETT: *(In a voice we have never heard)* Give That Back Now.

(Beat. FRANKLIN FISKE *holds out the button to* LOUISA BARRETT.*)*

FRANKLIN FISKE: I hope I never get called into your office.

*(*LOUISA BARRETT *looks at the button in* FRANKLIN FISKE's *hand.)*

LOUISA BARRETT: Keep it if you like. I'd forgotten it was there.

FRANKLIN FISKE: Did you know Cleveland when he lived here?

LOUISA BARRETT: He was gone before I came.

FRANKLIN FISKE: I'm surprised. That you, as a lady, I mean—

LOUISA BARRETT: You mean his private life.

FRANKLIN FISKE: President Cleveland's private life is hardly a topic for ladies.

LOUISA BARRETT: Yes, the Maria Halpin business.

FRANKLIN FISKE: "Ma, Ma, where's my Pa?"

LOUISA BARRETT: "Gone to the White House, ha ha ha!"

FRANKLIN FISKE: Most politicians settle for *kissing* babies. They don't wander around making them.

LOUISA BARRETT: Don't they?

FRANKLIN FISKE: Miss Barrett, you shock me.

LOUISA BARRETT: At least he admitted it. He was more honest than most.

FRANKLIN FISKE: And committing Maria Halpin to an insane asylum till she gave the baby up for adoption, that had an honest directness about it, yes. Must have been quite a deterrent to other women in her position.

LOUISA BARRETT: Yes. All that, yes. Here in Buffalo we remember when he was mayor, and put a stop to bribery and corruption.

FRANKLIN FISKE: And then he went to the White House as a reformer and sent in troops to put down the Pullman strike. And sat on his hands while people starved in the depression of '93. How can you keep the souvenir of a man whose only creed was that a president has no authority to interfere with anything that happens in the country he happens to be president of?

LOUISA BARRETT: Yes, all right, I was a fool. He betrayed my ideals—and his own.

FRANKLIN FISKE: But you still carry his button.

LOUISA BARRETT: As I said, I'd forgotten it was there.

FRANKLIN FISKE: It's not that large a reticule, and it's not that small a button. If you still care about bribery and corruption, help me.

LOUISA BARRETT: You want me to betray my friends.

FRANKLIN FISKE: I want you to help your country. The utilities should belong to the people.

LOUISA BARRETT: As Mr Fitzhugh pointed out, the state of New York has given the company the right to use the water—

FRANKLIN FISKE: And as Mr Bates pointed out, somebody's palms were greased to manage that. The water of the Great Lakes belongs to all the people, not just the people wealthy enough to exploit it. That means you and me.

LOUISA BARRETT: I know nothing of these matters.

FRANKLIN FISKE: Yes, you do, you know you do. These men have accepted you. They let down their guard with you, speak of things they would never say in front of someone like me. Because they do not think that you could possibly understand. Isn't that a fact? I haven't told anyone what I'm doing here, only you. Just tell me what you hear.

LOUISA BARRETT: I've been fooled by reformers before. I'm sorry.

FRANKLIN FISKE: But, Miss Barrett, surely—

LOUISA BARRETT: I have loyalties to this place!

GRACE SINCLAIR: *(Off)* Violets! I want to pick some for Mama!

LOUISA BARRETT: A man like you, a life like yours, you can't know what that means.

(GRACE SINCLAIR *runs through, dressed for snow.*)

(FRANKLIN FISKE *exits.* LOUISA BARRETT *remains.*)

Scene 10:
Forest Lawn

(THOMAS SINCLAIR *enters, dressed for snow. During the scene, other people stroll past from time to time.*)

THOMAS SINCLAIR: I'm glad you could come along today.

LOUISA BARRETT: I haven't taken a sleigh ride for fun in…since I was Grace's age.

THOMAS SINCLAIR: She seems more contented, don't you think? She isn't…the way she sometimes gets. The drawing lessons are good.

LOUISA BARRETT: Drawing lessons?

THOMAS SINCLAIR: I engaged your Miss Riley. I thought she'd have told you.

LOUISA BARRETT: And Grace is doing well?

THOMAS SINCLAIR: Keeps her busy, that's what matters.

LOUISA BARRETT: Tom. Something has been…troubling me.

THOMAS SINCLAIR: Tell me.

LOUISA BARRETT: It's just…I was surprised, after Karl Speyer was…after he died. I mean, that you didn't…

THOMAS SINCLAIR: That I didn't tell the police he came to the house that evening? That we argued?

LOUISA BARRETT: Yes.

THOMAS SINCLAIR: You must have been troubled for weeks now.

LOUISA BARRETT: Yes.

THOMAS SINCLAIR: Have you talked to anyone about your troubles?

LOUISA BARRETT: Of course not.

THOMAS SINCLAIR: You should have come to me.

LOUISA BARRETT: I felt shy.

THOMAS SINCLAIR: Shy? You?

LOUISA BARRETT: I'm very shy. Once you get to know me.

THOMAS SINCLAIR: I didn't tell anyone about Speyer's visit because it's irrelevant. I'm trying to run a business, and I can't do it with police and reporters swarming over me. Speyer and I had probably had that argument five times before.

LOUISA BARRETT: There are people saying you arranged his death.

THOMAS SINCLAIR: No one I know, I hope.

LOUISA BARRETT: Of course not. But then you gave all that money to the school, and...people wondered.

THOMAS SINCLAIR: People.

LOUISA BARRETT: Just people.

THOMAS SINCLAIR: Speyer's death was an accident. That's what the coroner's going to rule.

LOUISA BARRETT: Was that in the newspapers?

THOMAS SINCLAIR: It will be. Old Dexter Rumsey sent me a message. Said he thought I'd like to know.

LOUISA BARRETT: Thought you'd like to know the ruling? Or that he already knows what the ruling is going to be?

THOMAS SINCLAIR: I didn't know you had such a head for business.

GRACE SINCLAIR: *(Joining them, holding violets)* Mama loved the snow.

LOUISA BARRETT: Yes.

GRACE SINCLAIR: I pretend she visits me sometimes. Watch. I spin around really fast like this— *(Demonstrating)* —and I can see her in the corner of my eye, just like she's standing there! *(Stopping)* Did you see her?

THOMAS SINCLAIR: No, darling. We didn't see her.

GRACE SINCLAIR: Neither did I. Look, there's Winifred Coatsworth! Winnie! *(She runs out.)*

THOMAS SINCLAIR: Lord, it's hard to keep up.

LOUISA BARRETT: *(Distracted)* Mm.

(Because among the strolling passersby is MARGARET SINCLAIR, *dressed for snow and holding a deeply bundled baby.)*

MARGARET SINCLAIR: Who's got the best baby? Who's got the best baby? Oh, Louisa, bless you for finding her.

THOMAS SINCLAIR: I've been thinking a lot about her mother.

LOUISA BARRETT: Margaret must be so alive in your mind.

(As MARGARET SINCLAIR *drifts away among the other passersby:)*

THOMAS SINCLAIR: Not Margaret. Grace's real mother. Nobody ever saw her but you.

LOUISA BARRETT: I told you everything I knew. I met her in New York City.

THOMAS SINCLAIR: Poor girl, dear God, seduced by— what did she tell you?

LOUISA BARRETT: Her brother-in-law.

THOMAS SINCLAIR: Was that a lie, do you think?

LOUISA BARRETT: What—who—

THOMAS SINCLAIR: The girl, if it was really the groom, or a servant—

LOUISA BARRETT: Strange that you're thinking about all this now.

THOMAS SINCLAIR: Remember how Margaret dressed up like she was having it herself? No, you wouldn't remember, you were away on sabbatical, weren't you? Well, Dr. Perlmutter made house calls, brought padding she could wear, bigger every time.

LOUISA BARRETT: So you weren't the first couple with a secret like this.

THOMAS SINCLAIR: He came that night to deliver the baby. And he did, he delivered the baby from New York!

LOUISA BARRETT: Shh.

THOMAS SINCLAIR: I wanted to tell people, she's better than some ordinary baby, she's a miracle. That's why we called her Grace.

LOUISA BARRETT: But there's a stigma.

THOMAS SINCLAIR: I know. What's wrong with us, that we needed a miracle. You know, something's been troubling me, too.

LOUISA BARRETT: What?

THOMAS SINCLAIR: I hesitated to bring it up, but since you've practically accused me of murder, well, that does break the ice.

LOUISA BARRETT: Tom—

THOMAS SINCLAIR: I've been keeping a closer eye on Grace. Bringing work home, going over papers in my library, that sort of thing. She's been joining me, drawing, doing her homework. More and more she reminds me of someone. Of you, in fact.

LOUISA BARRETT: Tom, while Margaret was alive, she was the most important influence on Grace, but now, well, it's natural she would look to me—to any of her teachers, older girls—if you knew them as you do me, you'd see them in her manner, as well—

THOMAS SINCLAIR: Not her manner. Her features. I keep thinking I see you in her, and her in you. What does that mean, do you think?

(Beat)

LOUISA BARRETT: That it's terrible when friends start to wonder about each other?

THOMAS SINCLAIR: That's what I thought it meant. After all, if you can't trust your friends…

GRACE SINCLAIR: *(Off)* Papa! Come see!

*(*THOMAS SINCLAIR *exits.)*

LOUISA BARRETT: How true.

*(*LOUISA BARRETT *remains, as the lights and in fact the decade change:)*

Scene 11:
184 Delaware

(Enter MARIA LOVE, *escorting former president* GROVER CLEVELAND, *joined by party guests:* RICHARD WATSON GILDER, JOHN J ALBRIGHT, JOHN MILBURN, DEXTER RUMSEY. *Hurriedly, a little behind as usual,* THOMAS SINCLAIR *enters, lending an arm to* MARGARET SINCLAIR.)*

MARIA LOVE: Ladies and gentlemen. Join me in welcoming home, as he begins what I know will be his triumphal march back to the White House in 1892, Buffalo's favorite son—

JOHN J ALBRIGHT: *(Quietly)* Prodigal Son…

MARIA LOVE: Our Once and Future King…Steven Grover Cleveland.

(Applause and calls for "Speech! Speech!")

GROVER CLEVELAND: Miss Love, folks, this means a lot. Rumsey, Albright. Let's be honest here for a moment. I know that when I was in the White House, some folks here in Buffalo didn't get everything they deserved.

(Cries of "No! No!")

GROVER CLEVELAND: And some folks were lucky they *didn't* get what they deserved!

(Laughter, with an edge)

GROVER CLEVELAND: But that's water under the bridge, eh? Water over the Falls. This city—our city—is united and strong. And when I get back in the White House, we'll really have the chance to show the country how we do things here in Buffalo!

(Applause, and a rush to shake hands and slap backs.)

MARIA LOVE: Miss Barrett, good evening.

LOUISA BARRETT: Miss Love. It was so kind of you to invite us Macaulay teachers.

MARIA LOVE: Not the Macaulay teachers, Miss Barrett. Just you.

LOUISA BARRETT: Really? I—

MARIA LOVE: We have noticed what you have done for the school, my dear. You are being groomed.

LOUISA BARRETT: My goodness.

DEXTER RUMSEY: Evening, Miss Love.

MARIA LOVE: Mr Rumsey. You remember—

DEXTER RUMSEY: Miss…Barrett. I'm so glad you could come.

MARIA LOVE: *(Heading for the president)* I must return to my duties.

DEXTER RUMSEY: Of course. Enjoying yourself, Miss Barrett?

LOUISA BARRETT: I'm honored to be here.

DEXTER RUMSEY: Have you met the president?

LOUISA BARRETT: Oh, no, I—

DEXTER RUMSEY: You should. I know young people do enjoy such things. I myself am feeling a bit beyond presidents. But come along. Mr President!

GROVER CLEVELAND: Rumsey!

DEXTER RUMSEY: May I present Miss Louisa Barrett? A teacher—a jewel among our faculty at the Macaulay School for Girls.

GROVER CLEVELAND: Charmed, Miss Barrett.

LOUISA BARRETT: Mr President. It's an honor to meet you.

GROVER CLEVELAND: One of the best perquisites of my old job, Rumsey, lovely young persons are honored to meet a fella.

LOUISA BARRETT: Sir, I meant it was an honor to meet the man who told Congress that industry should be serving the people instead of vice versa. That "trusts and corporations were becoming the people's masters…their fortunes built on undue exactions from the masses."

GROVER CLEVELAND: Well now.

DEXTER RUMSEY: *(Drifting away)* I see you have no need of me…

GROVER CLEVELAND: And you're an Educator, Miss Barrett.

LOUISA BARRETT: That sounds a little grander than it—

GROVER CLEVELAND: Oh, it is grand. Most powerful job in the world, isn't it.

LOUISA BARRETT: It…sometimes, sir.

GROVER CLEVELAND: Absolutely. Influence. Influence over how people think.

LOUISA BARRETT: I see what you mean, sir.

GROVER CLEVELAND: I try to influence how people vote, what people do. It's hopeless.

LOUISA BARRETT: Hopeless, no—

GROVER CLEVELAND: Unless you can influence how they think. How they think about themselves. Their position in the world.

LOUISA BARRETT: I see what you mean, sir.

GROVER CLEVELAND: So, Education: how are we doing?

LOUISA BARRETT: We?

GROVER CLEVELAND: As a nation.

LOUISA BARRETT: Oh. You're asking me?

GROVER CLEVELAND: Teach me.

LOUISA BARRETT: Oh. Well. Our girls are underserved. Especially in the physical sciences.

GROVER CLEVELAND: Gilder!

LOUISA BARRETT: I should—

GROVER CLEVELAND: You're right—

LOUISA BARRETT: Sir, it's been—

GROVER CLEVELAND: This is no place for a real conversation. Would you care to continue this later?

LOUISA BARRETT: Oh. Sir, I—

GROVER CLEVELAND: Leave it to me. We don't want any jealousies, though. Or anyone tagging along?

LOUISA BARRETT: I…see what you mean.

GROVER CLEVELAND: So. Our secret? Go off now and talk to your friends, I'll have someone fetch you. Milburn, you dog!

(GROVER CLEVELAND *wanders away, gathering people around him. He exits during the following.*)

THOMAS SINCLAIR: Louisa. I think I should get Margaret home.

LOUISA BARRETT: Is she all right?

MARGARET SINCLAIR: Just tired still.

THOMAS SINCLAIR: I'll get your cloaks, shall I?

LOUISA BARRETT: I think I'll stay for a bit.

THOMAS SINCLAIR: You're sure? *(He exits.)*

LOUISA BARRETT: But you're all right?

MARGARET SINCLAIR: Sad, mostly. And now Dr Perlmutter says I can't keep trying, next time it could be me and the baby both.

LOUISA BARRETT: Sweetheart. Please be careful of yourself.

MARGARET SINCLAIR: Oh, Tom's been an angel of patience. Haven't you, love?

THOMAS SINCLAIR: Haven't I what? I'm sure I have, whatever it is. Good night, Louisa.

(LOUISA BARRETT and MARGARET SINCLAIR embrace. The SINCLAIRS exit. As if on cue, RICHARD WATSON GILDER crosses to LOUISA BARRETT, holding her cloak.)

RICHARD WATSON GILDER: Miss Barrett?

LOUISA BARRETT: Yes?

RICHARD WATSON GILDER: Are you ready to go?

LOUISA BARRETT: Oh. Yes, of course.

(As RICHARD WATSON GILDER helps LOUISA BARRETT on with her cloak, the rest of the party exits and the lights change.)

RICHARD WATSON GILDER: We'll go in the back entrance. If I were you, I'd place your shawl over your head.

(LOUISA BARRETT does so.)

RICHARD WATSON GILDER: And here we are.

(The lights continue to change, to:)

Scene 12:
Iroquois Hotel

(LOUISA BARRETT and RICHARD WATSON GILDER stand listening for a moment.)

GROVER CLEVELAND: *(Singing quietly, off)*
There's a log in the hole at the bottom of the sea…
There's a log in the hole at the bottom of the sea…
There's a hole, there's a hole, there's a hole in the bottom of the sea…

RICHARD WATSON GILDER: *(Reaching for her cloak)* I can take that if you like. I don't think anyone saw you. *(Calling)* Sir?

(Helping LOUISA BARRETT off with the cloak:)

RICHARD WATSON GILDER: You look fine.

GROVER CLEVELAND: *(Singing quietly, off)*
There's a bump on the log in the hole in the bottom of the sea…

RICHARD WATSON GILDER: *(Calling)* Sir? I'll be leaving now.

(RICHARD WATSON GILDER exits, carrying the cloak. GROVER CLEVELAND enters, wearing a silk dressing gown.)

GROVER CLEVELAND: *(Singing quietly)*
There's a bump on the log in the…
Well. Hello again.

LOUISA BARRETT: Hello, sir.

GROVER CLEVELAND: You certainly are a beauty.

LOUISA BARRETT: Oh. Thank you.

*(*Grover Cleveland *kisses* Louisa Barrett. *She tries to push him away.)*

Louisa Barrett: What are you doing?

Grover Cleveland: Playful, eh?

Louisa Barrett: I'd better go. This isn't—

*(*Grover Cleveland *presses* Louisa Barrett *close.)*

Grover Cleveland: What lovely eyes you have. Hazel, eh?

Louisa Barrett: I'd better go.

Grover Cleveland: Now, now, dear. Don't be like that.

Louisa Barrett: Please. I didn't know—

Grover Cleveland: You don't have to do that. I'm a straightforward fella. Some men like a woman to pretend she doesn't know. That's not for me. Now.

Louisa Barrett: Please. I'm not that kind of—

*(*Louisa Barrett *struggles, and* Grover Cleveland *holds her wrists.)*

Grover Cleveland: Oh, I hate to see a bright woman play dumb. I've got a lot to do tomorrow, and I'm too old to spend the night pretending to assault your pretended virtue.

Louisa Barrett: I'm not. Playing dumb. Please let me go.

*(*Grover Cleveland *does.)*

Grover Cleveland: All right, now, honestly. Where do you want to go? Mm? Down the hall and into the lobby of the Iroquois Hotel? At this hour? Reporters are still down there. You don't really want that. *(Touching her)* You want to be here, or you wouldn't be here. You want to do this, because this is what gets done here. You are that kind of woman, because only that kind of woman would have come.

LOUISA BARRETT: I didn't know. Why didn't I know.

GROVER CLEVELAND: *(Putting his arms around her)* You stay now, and I'll make sure you get home safely.

LOUISA BARRETT: Couldn't I just...stay here? Without...

GROVER CLEVELAND: No. That would be stupid and indecisive. We're not stupid and indecisive, are we? *(Kissing away a tear)* Good girl.

(GROVER CLEVELAND kisses LOUISA BARRETT's mouth. She turns away.)

GROVER CLEVELAND: Still shy?

(Holding LOUISA BARRETT tightly, GROVER CLEVELAND propels her toward the exit. She struggles one more time.)

GROVER CLEVELAND: Too late for that now. And really, my dear, it will be our secret.

(The lights fade.)

END OF ACT ONE

ACT TWO

Scene 1:
Niagara Falls

(The roar of the Falls. Louisa Barrett *and* Franklin Fiske, *in oilskins, shouting.)*

Franklin Fiske: Is it different?

Louisa Barrett: What?

Franklin Fiske: Is it different?

Louisa Barrett: Is what different?

Franklin Fiske: The Falls. Because of the water they're taking out.

Louisa Barrett: No, nothing's changed.

Franklin Fiske: What more could Daniel Henry Bates want, anyway? This is plenty transcendent for me.

(Off Louisa Barrett'*s look:)*

Franklin Fiske: What are you laughing at?

Louisa Barrett: *(Pointing)* Rainbows. Circles, on your face.

Franklin Fiske: Yours too.

(The lights fade to plain daylight. The roar recedes.)

Scene 2:
Three Sisters Islands

(JAMES FITZHUGH *enters, gazing and humming. Birdsong and flowing water.*)

JAMES FITZHUGH: *(Singing quietly)*
I will not cease from mental fight,
Nor shall my sword sleep in my hand,
Till we have built Jerusalem...

(LOUISA BARRETT *and* FRANKLIN FISKE *join* JAMES FITZHUGH.)

FRANKLIN FISKE: Say! Mr Fitzhugh, isn't it?

JAMES FITZHUGH: Um. Yes.

FRANKLIN FISKE: Franklin Fiske. I heard you speak at Lyric Hall. Very edifying.

JAMES FITZHUGH: How do you do.

FRANKLIN FISKE: And this is Miss Louisa Barrett.

JAMES FITZHUGH: Mr Sinclair's friend.

LOUISA BARRETT: How do you do, Mr Fitzhugh. I'm surprised to find you here at Niagara.

JAMES FITZHUGH: Oh, I love it here.

LOUISA BARRETT: I thought Mr Sinclair had you all working 'round the clock to open the new powerhouse in time for President McKinley.

JAMES FITZHUGH: I walk here on my lunch hour, whenever I can. *(Checking his watch)* Oh, and in fact if you'll excuse me...

LOUISA BARRETT: Of course.

FRANKLIN FISKE: Mr Fitzhugh, may we speak sometime? I'm very interested in your work.

JAMES FITZHUGH: Of course, call the office. Um, nice to have met you. *(He exits.)*

LOUISA BARRETT: What are you up to?

FRANKLIN FISKE: Oh, the usual. The water is so calm.

LOUISA BARRETT: So it seems.

FRANKLIN FISKE: I feel like I could wade in it. I'd like to, in fact. Perhaps I will!

LOUISA BARRETT: Please don't. The current is tricky.

FRANKLIN FISKE: Oh, yes. So your father said.

LOUISA BARRETT: I wouldn't want to lose you.

FRANKLIN FISKE: Hmm. May I take your picture? I could go get the camera.

LOUISA BARRETT: Franklin, what are you going to do with all your pictures?

FRANKLIN FISKE: Well, I do need to keep up my disguise. When I get a big pile of them, I'll ask John J Albright to give me an exhibition at his new art museum. You can recommend me.

LOUISA BARRETT: You're incorrigible.

FRANKLIN FISKE: Thank you—my specialty.

(FRANKLIN FISKE *exits.* LOUISA BARRETT *watches the water.*)

GRACE SINCLAIR: *(Off)* Aunt Louisa!

(GRACE SINCLAIR *and* SUSANNAH RILEY *enter, with art supplies.*)

LOUISA BARRETT: Grace! What are you doing here?

GRACE SINCLAIR: Miss Riley and I came here on the train.

LOUISA BARRETT: Did you know the train is run with electricity from your Papa's power station?

GRACE SINCLAIR: Yes, I know.

SUSANNAH RILEY: Show Miss Barrett what you've been doing, Grace.

GRACE SINCLAIR: *(Showing her painting)* I'm doing an oil painting! Look!

LOUISA BARRETT: You've made a fine start, Grace.

GRACE SINCLAIR: Show her yours, Miss Riley.

SUSANNAH RILEY: Well. *(She does so.)*

LOUISA BARRETT: This is extraordinary, Miss Riley.

SUSANNAH RILEY: Thank you. It's hard to capture the way the light bounces off the water onto the lower leaves of the trees. But that's the most beautiful part of being by the water.

LOUISA BARRETT: I see what you mean.

SUSANNAH RILEY: Do you? The reflections, you see, every bit of light is like a different facet—

GRACE SINCLAIR: Miss Barrett! This is the first time I've painted *en plein air*. That's French for "outside." And it's the first time I've used oils!

SUSANNAH RILEY: Grace Sinclair! Don't interrupt when adults are speaking, you know better.

GRACE SINCLAIR: Yes, Miss Riley.

LOUISA BARRETT: You've picked a fine subject for your first oil painting, Grace.

GRACE SINCLAIR: Aunt Louisa? Could we go home together on the train? All of us?

LOUISA BARRETT: Yes, Grace, that would be nice. Why don't you finish your work. Would you come with me a few paces, Miss Riley?

SUSANNAH RILEY: Of course. Grace, you work hard and surprise us with all you've done when we get back.

LOUISA BARRETT: Stay where we can see you!

(GRACE SINCLAIR *exits.*)

SUSANNAH RILEY: I always come out here on days like this.

LOUISA BARRETT: I'm glad to have a few minutes to talk with you alone. I haven't had a chance, since the debate at Lyric Hall.

SUSANNAH RILEY: You saw that I was with Mr Daniel Henry Bates.

LOUISA BARRETT: Yes.

SUSANNAH RILEY: I know you don't approve of my beliefs.

LOUISA BARRETT: You are not a child, Miss Riley. The best families in the city have invested in the power station. Do you think they will hire you to tutor their daughters, if they see you up in front of everyone, threatening the destruction of their investment? Isn't that what Mr Bates is threatening?

SUSANNAH RILEY: He has not confided in me.

LOUISA BARRETT: The city will assume that he has. Believe me. So you will have to decide, as do we all, which side you are on. Whatever your private beliefs may be. I am saying this for your own good.

SUSANNAH RILEY: Thank you, Miss Barrett. (*Beat*) It is beautiful though, isn't it?

LOUISA BARRETT: I haven't been here since I was a girl.

SUSANNAH RILEY: Is it different?

LOUISA BARRETT: The island seems larger.

SUSANNAH RILEY: Do you know why?

LOUISA BARRETT: The water they're taking from the river. You can see the difference.

SUSANNAH RILEY: Yes.

LOUISA BARRETT: Well. There's still enough for purposes of transcendence.

SUSANNAH RILEY: Do you see how each tilt of a wave catches a different reflection? A sky or a cloud or a tree reflected in each one. *(Stepping forward)* That's never really been captured in the paintings of Niagara—that it's so many different pictures. *(Taking another step forward)* Sometimes I want to wade in and touch those pictures. To be part of them. To let the water carry me on its back.

LOUISA BARRETT: The river water's filled with air— that's what gives it the color.

SUSANNAH RILEY: Sometimes I want to float there. The air in the water would hold me up.

(LOUISA BARRETT has followed SUSANNAH RILEY to the water.)

SUSANNAH RILEY: Do you ever want to float there? Imagine. The water lifting your body and carrying you away. No need to fight for anything. No right or wrong.

(LOUISA BARRETT steps past SUSANNAH RILEY, further into the water.)

SUSANNAH RILEY: Just resting. The water is like God, isn't it?

(FRANKLIN FISKE enters.)

FRANKLIN FISKE: Louisa!

LOUISA BARRETT: *(Starting back)* What—is everything all right?

FRANKLIN FISKE: Is the girl here? Get the girl.

LOUISA BARRETT: Grace!

SUSANNAH RILEY: Grace!

LOUISA BARRETT: What is it, Franklin?

FRANKLIN FISKE: I've just heard—James Fitzhugh has been found in the gorge. He seems to have been swept over the Falls.

LOUISA BARRETT: Oh my God. Grace!

(GRACE SINCLAIR *enters, carrying her portfolio.*)

GRACE SINCLAIR: There you are. I was looking for you.

LOUISA BARRETT: *(Almost rushing to embrace her)* Grace, you're all right?

GRACE SINCLAIR: Of course I am. You got your boots wet. That's not fair, I want cool feet, too, I'm going to—

LOUISA BARRETT, SUSANNAH RILEY & FRANKLIN FISKE: No!

(GRACE SINCLAIR *stops.*)

FRANKLIN FISKE: Miss Riley? Why don't we gather the tools of our trades?

SUSANNAH RILEY: Yes.

(FRANKLIN FISKE *and* SUSANNAH RILEY *exit.*)

GRACE SINCLAIR: What's wrong with everybody?

LOUISA BARRETT: Everything's fine.

GRACE SINCLAIR: Who was that man?

LOUISA BARRETT: May I look at your drawings, Grace?

GRACE SINCLAIR: All right. Were you and Miss Riley—

LOUISA BARRETT: We're fine. We'll go to the train any minute now.

(LOUISA BARRETT *and* GRACE SINCLAIR *leaf through* GRACE SINCLAIR'*s portfolio.*)

GRACE SINCLAIR: Guess what?

LOUISA BARRETT: What.

GRACE SINCLAIR: I have a secret that you don't know.

LOUISA BARRETT: That's what makes it a secret. That's very good of your cat.

GRACE SINCLAIR: See if you can guess. It's something Papa and I were talking about last night.

LOUISA BARRETT: That's something I could never guess.

GRACE SINCLAIR: He asked me if it would be all right if he began— *(In her Irish accent)* —courting a lady.

LOUISA BARRETT: Do you know who the lady is?

GRACE SINCLAIR: *(Herself again)* You, of course.

LOUISA BARRETT: Did he say it was me?

GRACE SINCLAIR: He didn't have to say it, I knew it.

LOUISA BARRETT: Grace. It could be anyone. It could be Miss Riley, for all we know.

GRACE SINCLAIR: It can't be Miss Riley, she's too young to marry Papa! You're our best friend—

LOUISA BARRETT: Well, thank you, Grace.

GRACE SINCLAIR: You're my godmother, you were Mama's friend—

LOUISA BARRETT: I don't think he was talking about me, Grace.

GRACE SINCLAIR: But there isn't anyone else. *(Looking after* FRANKLIN FISKE*)* Do you like that man?

LOUISA BARRETT: I'm already your godmother.

GRACE SINCLAIR: But—

LOUISA BARRETT: That will never change, no matter what.

GRACE SINCLAIR: And now you'll be my mother! Just like my real mother!

(Beat)

LOUISA BARRETT: I would be. Yes. I would.

GRACE SINCLAIR: You won't say I told, will you?

LOUISA BARRETT: No, Grace, I won't tell, it will be our secret. I see Miss Riley has you doing portraits, too. This is a good one of your father.

GRACE SINCLAIR: That's in his library. We work together there sometimes.

LOUISA BARRETT: He told me. *(Turning a page)* What are these, now? Multiplication tables? All these numbers and dollars…

GRACE SINCLAIR: Oh. Nothing.

LOUISA BARRETT: "Inspection." This is something of your father's. Where did you get this?

GRACE SINCLAIR: I was working with Papa at his desk. That's when I made that picture of him. These must have gotten mixed in by mistake.

LOUISA BARRETT: You'll return them right away.

GRACE SINCLAIR: I promise.

(GRACE SINCLAIR runs off. LOUISA BARRETT watches her go as around her the scene changes:)

Scene 3:
The Twentieth Century Club

LOUISA BARRETT: I'm afraid for the girl.

(MARY TALBERT enters and listens.)

LOUISA BARRETT: I keep coming back to that. If the other students resent my decision, they will not take it out on me. They will, in great and small ways, many without the least awareness, make your niece's life a hell. Has her life prepared her for that kind of opposition?

MARY TALBERT: I believe it has prepared her. And if it hasn't, she'd better get prepared.

LOUISA BARRETT: Even the poorer white girls have found it a challenge so great that I wonder if the benefits outweigh the hardships.

MARY TALBERT: But you have been one such poor girl yourself.

LOUISA BARRETT: My father was a college professor.

MARY TALBERT: Yes, a hired hand, to girls like these.

LOUISA BARRETT: I suppose.

MARY TALBERT: And you have survived and thrived. Do you regret the opportunities you have made such use of?

LOUISA BARRETT: I had no choice. I had to support myself.

MARY TALBERT: We all have choices. For some the range of choice is wider than for others. But no one has none.

LOUISA BARRETT: I fear for her. I would not have it on my conscience to put an unprepared young person into a position of so little power. The cruelty…

MARY TALBERT: Something terrible must have happened to you, Miss Barrett. I am sorry. But do not impose your fears on this girl. My niece is ready to stand up for herself and for what she believes is right. Can you say the same? Challenge these men. Dare them to dismiss you. You may be surprised to find them reluctant to turn you away. You may finally discover your value to the community.

LOUISA BARRETT: I would like to help, truly I would, but—

MARY TALBERT: But your job is too precious? If you were dismissed, other cities would snap you up, for the very independence you had shown. There are schools for girls in many cities.

LOUISA BARRETT: I cannot go to another city.

MARY TALBERT: So. Something personal holds you back. Woe to us all when we let the personal hold sway over the fight for justice. Do you think I haven't wondered: maybe it would have been better to stay in the background, out of everyone's way. I've had to make myself so harsh for the work. Sometimes I sound sanctimonious even to myself. I've had to make my body into a shield, or I could never get up on soapboxes and shout at people.

LOUISA BARRETT: You could never hide away. Your choice has been the opposite of mine. You were right.

MARY TALBERT: What's holding you back? Something keeps you here in Buffalo, and holds you back. Some secret, I think. Shall I guess?

LOUISA BARRETT: Guess all you like.

MARY TALBERT: I have no evidence. But I've allowed myself a speculation.

LOUISA BARRETT: Indeed.

MARY TALBERT: Here is what I've decided: a long time ago, you fell in love with a man. You were reckless. He couldn't marry you for whatever reason. You paid the price. You bore a child. Even I understand what love can make a woman do.

LOUISA BARRETT: I never fell in love with a man.

MARY TALBERT: Oh. I see. I'm sorry. Was he a stranger? *(Beat)* I understand. *(Beat)* If that child could see you— and maybe she can—what kind of person would you want her to see? Wouldn't you want her to say to herself, "I wish I had a mother like that." Any fool can have a child in this life. It's something else to be the kind of person a child wants to have in her life. You have it in you to be that kind of person. But you have to stand up.

(The scene changes.)

Scene 4:
Pan-American Exposition

*(*JOHN MILBURN *escorts vice president* THEODORE ROOSEVELT *and party, including* RICHARD WATSON GILDER, JOHN J ALBRIGHT, *and, at his own pace,* DEXTER RUMSEY. They are met by THOMAS SINCLAIR, a little rushed as always, with GRACE SINCLAIR.)*

JOHN MILBURN: Right this way, Mr Vice President. Here we have the crown, the coup, the *piece de resistance* of the Pan-American Exposition…the Electric Tower!

(A sudden blaze of electric light)

THEODORE ROOSEVELT: Isn't this fine, now! Really putting the electricity through its paces.

JOHN MILBURN: And here's the man we have to thank. Vice President Roosevelt, may I introduce Mr Thomas Sinclair?

THEODORE ROOSEVELT: The hydroelectric fella! Been following that! Damn fine job!

THOMAS SINCLAIR: Thank you, sir.

THEODORE ROOSEVELT: Think you'll have that third powerhouse ready for my boss to take her online come September?

THOMAS SINCLAIR: I think so, sir.

THEODORE ROOSEVELT: Bully!

THOMAS SINCLAIR: May I present Miss Louisa Barrett.

THEODORE ROOSEVELT: Charmed!

LOUISA BARRETT: Sir.

THOMAS SINCLAIR: And this is my daughter, Grace.

THEODORE ROOSEVELT: I saw you in the Electrical Building, hiding behind the coats. Nothing escapes me! Fine thing in a girl, an interest in the future. Keep it up! Eh, Gilder? A fine thing, for a girl to care about the future.

RICHARD WATSON GILDER: Yes, sir.

THEODORE ROOSEVELT: Know these people, Gilder?

RICHARD WATSON GILDER: I met Miss Barrett during a previous—

THEODORE ROOSEVELT: The big fella here is Tom Sinclair, head of the power station and a damn fine job he's doing with it too. And this is his daughter, who's training to be an electrical engineer.

RICHARD WATSON GILDER: Sir, we should—

THEODORE ROOSEVELT: Sinclair! Tell me about this stepping-down process for alternating current.

THOMAS SINCLAIR: Well, sir…

(THEODORE ROOSEVELT *takes* THOMAS SINCLAIR *by the elbow and they stroll away, talking.*)

RICHARD WATSON GILDER: (*To* LOUISA BARRETT) My, my, it's almost, what, ten years since we met, Miss Barrett? How well I recall it. When our esteemed former president Mr Cleveland was between terms. A time of upheaval.

LOUISA BARRETT: Yes.

RICHARD WATSON GILDER: You are as lovely as I remember. Lovelier, in fact. And you've come so far and accomplished so much. My friends here report back to me on your every activity! They sing your praises, but I reveal nothing!

LOUISA BARRETT: You are too kind.

RICHARD WATSON GILDER: Oh—isn't that Dexter Rumsey? Mr Rumsey!

DEXTER RUMSEY: Miss Barrett.

LOUISA BARRETT: Mr Rumsey. Do you know—?

RICHARD WATSON GILDER: Oh, Mr Rumsey and I met during a previous administration.

DEXTER RUMSEY: Of course. Good to see you again.

RICHARD WATSON GILDER: It's a wonderful thing, when a beautiful woman brings intelligent men together.

DEXTER RUMSEY: Indeed.

THEODORE ROOSEVELT: To the boats!

RICHARD WATSON GILDER: Would you excuse me, I must accompany the vice president to the reception. I trust I'll see you there.

(RICHARD WATSON GILDER *exits after* THEODORE ROOSEVELT *and others.*)

DEXTER RUMSEY: All this hoopla. The exposition, the vice president...

LOUISA BARRETT: The vice president seems very interested in hydroelectric power.

DEXTER RUMSEY: The vice president must be fueled by hydroelectric power. I preferred our city when it was staid and boring and we could concentrate on really important things, like business. And then on top of everything the deaths of Speyer and Fitzhugh to deal with.

LOUISA BARRETT: "Deal with"?

DEXTER RUMSEY: Anything dramatic comes under my purview, I'm afraid.

LOUISA BARRETT: Don't you believe both deaths were accidental?

DEXTER RUMSEY: Of course. So the coroner tells me.

JOHN J ALBRIGHT: Mr Rumsey. Miss Barrett.

LOUISA BARRETT: Mr Albright.

JOHN J ALBRIGHT: I think your people were looking for you, sir, you're supposed to be minding some duchesses or something.

DEXTER RUMSEY: Duty calls. *(He exits.)*

JOHN J ALBRIGHT: Miss Barrett. Did you ever happen to give my message to Sinclair?

LOUISA BARRETT: Yes, I did.

JOHN J ALBRIGHT: Really? What was his reaction?

LOUISA BARRETT: He laughed.

JOHN J ALBRIGHT: Oh.

LOUISA BARRETT: Mr Albright, what exactly—

JOHN J ALBRIGHT: Well, such is life. Grace! You are getting prettier all the time.

GRACE SINCLAIR: Thank you, Mr Albright.

THOMAS SINCLAIR: Albright!

JOHN J ALBRIGHT: Mr Sinclair. *(He exits.)*

LOUISA BARRETT: Tom, is everything—

THOMAS SINCLAIR: Are you going to the reception?

LOUISA BARRETT: I've long since lost any interest in political receptions. Are you going? I could see Grace home.

THOMAS SINCLAIR: Still not proper for me, party-going.

LOUISA BARRETT: Of course.

THOMAS SINCLAIR: Come back to the house. I see a few people—Peter! Peter Fronczyk! Come here, son!

(THOMAS SINCLAIR *exits, with* GRACE SINCLAIR *in tow.* FRANCESCA COATSWORTH *enters.)*

FRANCESCA COATSWORTH: Coming, Louisa? I've always wanted to see inside the Buffalo Club.

LOUISA BARRETT: You go on. I think I'll go with Mr Sinclair.

FRANCESCA COATSWORTH: Tom Sinclair's having his own little gathering? Now that takes nerve.

LOUISA BARRETT: A handful of people, Frannie. He's still in mourning, he can't go to receptions.

FRANCESCA COATSWORTH: He's saying he doesn't need us—Rumseys, Buffalo Club, anybody.

LOUISA BARRETT: You come too, to Tom's. Come along.

FRANCESCA COATSWORTH: No, no. I'll be off with the rest of the sheep. Louisa, listen…Dexter Rumsey, John Albright, the powers that be. They like you, they've made you one of them.

LOUISA BARRETT: I know.

FRANCESCA COATSWORTH: I don't think they're happy with Tom Sinclair. I think—well, I hear things, and I think he's got some kind of plans they don't like. Be careful who your friends are.

LOUISA BARRETT: You should tell that to Susannah Riley.

FRANCESCA COATSWORTH: I have. I can't get through to her either. I can't stop either one of you.

(FRANCESCA COATSWORTH *exits, along with the rest of the Exposition, as* THOMAS SINCLAIR, GRACE SINCLAIR, *and* PETER FRONCZYK *enter and the lights change.)*

THOMAS SINCLAIR: Before electricity, we would've had to close the exposition at sundown. Gives us a bit of a chance to serve the public, eh, Peter?

Scene 5:
Sinclairs'

(SERVANTS *bring on* SINCLAIRS' *terrace furniture, drinks.*)

PETER FRONCZYK: We should always serve the public, sir.

THOMAS SINCLAIR: Let's flatter ourselves that we do.

(LOUISA BARRETT *sits and* GRACE SINCLAIR *curls up in her lap.*)

THOMAS SINCLAIR: Well, here we are. A select group. You'll be completing your apprenticeship any day now, won't you, Peter? This young man is about to be a full-fledged board operator.

LOUISA BARRETT: Congratulations.

PETER FRONCZYK: Thank you.

THOMAS SINCLAIR: Too bad you're not farther along, I could use a new Chief Engineer. Nobody seems to want the job since poor Fitzhugh died. Having to do it myself for now. Takes me back. What are the men saying about Fitzhugh?

PETER FRONCZYK: What do you mean, sir?

THOMAS SINCLAIR: Do they think he might have walked into the water on purpose? Because of some upset at work?

PETER FRONCZYK: No, sir. Not at all. He never would have—

THOMAS SINCLAIR: Fine, fine. Anybody think it's
just a coincidence? Fitzhugh and Speyer? Couple of
accidents?

PETER FRONCZYK: Anything's possible, sir.

THOMAS SINCLAIR: That it is. That it is. Any other
explanations floating around? In my day they'd be
handicapping suspects by now. And running a pool on
who'll be next.

PETER FRONCZYK: There's nothing like that where I am,
sir.

THOMAS SINCLAIR: No? Come on, son. What odds are
they laying on me?

PETER FRONCZYK: I couldn't say, sir.

(Beat)

THOMAS SINCLAIR: Do you have any regrets? Leaving
your friends behind?

PETER FRONCZYK: My friends?

THOMAS SINCLAIR: Your colleagues. From the
International Brotherhood of Electrical Workers.

PETER FRONCZYK: I...well...

THOMAS SINCLAIR: Very reckless men. When I heard
they'd started stockpiling weapons—

PETER FRONCZYK: How did you—

THOMAS SINCLAIR: How am I supposed to do business
if I don't know what's going on! There are people
who'd love any excuse to send in the troops about
now. Do your friends know that?

PETER FRONCZYK: I think so.

THOMAS SINCLAIR: They'd better.

PETER FRONCZYK: I'd better be going.

THOMAS SINCLAIR: I remember your Da, Peter. Fine man. Bet you miss him.

PETER FRONCZYK: Yes, sir.

THOMAS SINCLAIR: When I was young, a man helped me along. Like a second father to me he was, back then.

PETER FRONCZYK: John J. Albright.

THOMAS SINCLAIR: John J. Albright. I ought to start doing the same. Let's you and me have a talk about that someday? Someday soon?

PETER FRONCZYK: All right, sir.

THOMAS SINCLAIR: Look at that girl, will you? Asleep in her party clothes. Louisa, would you help me get Grace into bed?

PETER FRONCZYK: Thank you, Mr Sinclair, for—

THOMAS SINCLAIR: No, thank you. Let's talk again.

(PETER FRONCZYK *exits.* THOMAS SINCLAIR *watches* LOUISA BARRETT *cradling* GRACE SINCLAIR.)

THOMAS SINCLAIR: Shall I move her?

(LOUISA BARRETT *shakes her head "no".)*

THOMAS SINCLAIR: You've been very quiet. Is everything all right?

(LOUISA BARRETT *nods.)*

THOMAS SINCLAIR: Louisa?

LOUISA BARRETT: I'm fine. I was just…even with everything…it's good to be here.

THOMAS SINCLAIR: 'Tis. I'm in a rare old mood… You know, Grace seems to have gotten a notion in her head that we should get married. Did you know?

(LOUISA BARRETT *nods.)*

THOMAS SINCLAIR: It's a pleasing thought. To be like this, always?

LOUISA BARRETT: You miss Margaret very much.

THOMAS SINCLAIR: It's not even a year.

LOUISA BARRETT: I know.

THOMAS SINCLAIR: I know you know. And, yes, part
of this is missing that life. But it's about you, as well.
You're all I could want in a mother for Grace. And
you're lovely, of course, I noticed that even when...
even before, if you'll forgive me saying so. And I feel I
know you. Do you think in a year or so we might have
an understanding with one another?

LOUISA BARRETT: Yes. I would agree to that.

THOMAS SINCLAIR: You would?

LOUISA BARRETT: Yes.

THOMAS SINCLAIR: Do you think possibly having an
understanding in a year or so will appease our little
girl?

LOUISA BARRETT: No.

THOMAS SINCLAIR: Neither do I. Well, that's part of
growing up, isn't it? Learning to wait for what you
want. In the meantime...

LOUISA BARRETT: Shh.

THOMAS SINCLAIR: I'll call one of the men to walk you
home. I shouldn't leave Grace.

(THOMAS SINCLAIR *picks up* GRACE SINCLAIR.)

LOUISA BARRETT: That's quite all right. I walk here all
the time.

THOMAS SINCLAIR: I'm sure you do, Louisa. But I'd
rather not take the risk.

(THOMAS SINCLAIR *exits, carrying* GRACE SINCLAIR. *As*
LOUISA BARRETT *watches them go, the lights change.)*

Scene 6:
Louisa Barrett's Office

SUSANNAH RILEY: Miss Barrett? *(She enters, carrying her drawing portfolio.)*

SUSANNAH RILEY: You know I tutor a few of the girls privately.

LOUISA BARRETT: Yes.

SUSANNAH RILEY: Yesterday I went to one girl's home for my regular visit. I had set her some work to do during the week. Figure drawing. She showed me these. *(Passing drawings)* I didn't feel I could mention it to her family and I didn't know who to turn to—

LOUISA BARRETT: What did you say when the girl showed these to you?

SUSANNAH RILEY: Well, I—I tried not at act surprised and I told her they were beautifully done and I asked her if she'd done them from life.

LOUISA BARRETT: And?

SUSANNAH RILEY: She said she had done them from memory.

LOUISA BARRETT: Not something she'd made up. Imagination.

SUSANNAH RILEY: Some of that...

LOUISA BARRETT: ... she couldn't have made up. No. How could she know.

SUSANNAH RILEY: What should we do?

LOUISA BARRETT: We must proceed cautiously. The girl is not the one at fault. The faces are shaded. Did you ask her who the people were?

SUSANNAH RILEY: Yes, she just giggled, she said it was an artistic secret.

LOUISA BARRETT: Artistic. Did you ask her what she thought the people were doing?

SUSANNAH RILEY: Yes. "Just resting." She said, "It was a rainy day."

LOUISA BARRETT: A rainy day.

SUSANNAH RILEY: Do you think she could have made it up somehow?

LOUISA BARRETT: It was a rainy day. That makes it sound very real, doesn't it. As if she's the one in the pictures?

SUSANNAH RILEY: Then she brought out some drawings of her cat. "This is my cat, cleaning her face." As if nothing had happened.

(Beat)

LOUISA BARRETT: It's Grace Sinclair, isn't it. The girl. It's Grace Sinclair.

SUSANNAH RILEY: I was afraid to say. But perhaps this explains some things.

(The roar of turbines. SUSANNAH RILEY *exits, leaving* LOUISA BARRETT *holding the drawings.)*

Scene 7:
Power station

*(*THOMAS SINCLAIR *enters and stands behind* LOUISA BARRETT, *looking at the drawings.)*

LOUISA BARRETT: We've got to try to discover who the man is. A servant, perhaps. Or a visitor brought in by the servants.

THOMAS SINCLAIR: Who did you say gave you these?

LOUISA BARRETT: Grace's art tutor. Susannah Riley. Or, or he's the older brother of one of Grace's—

THOMAS SINCLAIR: Don't be naïve. The man is supposed to be me.

LOUISA BARRETT: No!

THOMAS SINCLAIR: Today, of all days. Well, yes, obviously today. She's planned it very well.

LOUISA BARRETT: What do you mean?

THOMAS SINCLAIR: Grace had nothing to do with obscenities like these.

LOUISA BARRETT: You're telling me Susannah made them up?

THOMAS SINCLAIR: I think Susannah Riley did these drawings herself and brought them to you today so that you would rush out here to the power station to tell me. To distract me.

LOUISA BARRETT: Why would she do that?

THOMAS SINCLAIR: You don't know everything, Louisa, much as you like to think you do. Susannah Riley is a skilled artist, but she has also become a fanatic. You don't really believe this, do you? Of me? You think I would do such a thing?

LOUISA BARRETT: I'll talk to Grace.

THOMAS SINCLAIR: Louisa. Please don't.

LOUISA BARRETT: I have no choice.

THOMAS SINCLAIR: I would prefer my daughter not see such drawings.

LOUISA BARRETT: I'll believe Grace if she denies them.

THOMAS SINCLAIR: Louisa. Something will happen here tonight. It will prove what I'm saying. Stay and see for yourself.

LOUISA BARRETT: No, I am going to Grace.

THOMAS SINCLAIR: I can't let you go alone—and that's just what Susannah Riley's counting on, don't you see? She's expecting I'll return to town with you to set all this straight, and then she and her friends will have free rein here tonight. Can't you trust me for a few hours?

LOUISA BARRETT: What is supposed to happen?

THOMAS SINCLAIR: Mr Bates and his friends have gotten themselves some dynamite. They intend to blow up part of the powerhouse.

LOUISA BARRETT: What?

THOMAS SINCLAIR: I have to be here.

LOUISA BARRETT: Is it safe to stay?

THOMAS SINCLAIR: There's a risk, but I think the results will be worth it.

LOUISA BARRETT: I'll stay. But then I'll go to Grace.

THOMAS SINCLAIR: Come with me.

(LOUISA BARRETT *follows* THOMAS SINCLAIR *up the stairs as the lights and sound fade to night.*)

(*Moonlight through high windows. The transformers remain, huge dim presences.*)

(THOMAS SINCLAIR *and* LOUISA BARRETT *wait on a catwalk.*)

LOUISA BARRETT: Don't you have guards on duty?

THOMAS SINCLAIR: I sent them out. They'll come running when they hear the explosion. Now, when I tell you, follow me.

(*A beam of light from a lantern, off.*)

THOMAS SINCLAIR: Don't move.

*(The first man [*PETER FRONCZYK*] enters, with his back
to us, carrying a toolbox, and stops, listening. He gestures
behind him for others to come.)*

*(The next man enters slowly, and stops. He turns, taking
in the huge dim shapes and the roar. He is* DANIEL HENRY
BATES. *Then he gestures for others to come.)*

*(The first man has knelt and is working quickly and carefully
over his toolbox.)*

*(*SUSANNAH RILEY *enters, holding a lantern. another* MAN
*follows, a coil of rope slung over his shoulder, carrying a
truncheon. He joins the first man, crouching over their
work.)*

DANIEL HENRY BATES: *(Gazing up at the machinery,
transfixed)* Lo, I am come to Pandaemonium.

PETER FRONCZYK: Shh!

(The first man turns to look up at DANIEL HENRY BATES,
and we see his face: PETER FRONCZYK. *He stands, carefully,
holding a dynamite bomb.)*

DANIEL HENRY BATES: Peter?

*(*DANIEL HENRY BATES *holds out his hands, and* PETER
FRONCZYK *places the bomb in them. The other* MAN *has
picked up the toolbox.)*

PETER FRONCZYK: *(Pointing)* There's the Westinghouse-
Speyer.

SUSANNAH RILEY: Wait.

*(*SUSANNAH RILEY *listens. She opens the lantern and slowly
shines its beam around. Just as she's about to point it toward*
THOMAS SINCLAIR *and* LOUISA BARRETT—*)*

PETER FRONCZYK: Stop. The guards will see.

DANIEL HENRY BATES: Come. Show me the way, Peter.

*(*PETER FRONCZYK *leads the others off.)*

LOUISA BARRETT: How could they—

THOMAS SINCLAIR: Don't move.

LOUISA BARRETT: Aren't you going to stop them?

THOMAS SINCLAIR: Of course not.

(The saboteurs run through and out.)

THOMAS SINCLAIR: Now!

(THOMAS SINCLAIR takes LOUISA BARRETT's hand and they run for the stairs. Explosion. Lights out)

Scene 8:
Sinclairs'

(LOUISA BARRETT stands, in shock, as THOMAS SINCLAIR watches her.)

LOUISA BARRETT: I can't believe it. Peter Fronczyk. After all you were doing for him.

THOMAS SINCLAIR: Let's make sure Grace is asleep. Do you want to watch her?

LOUISA BARRETT: In a moment, let me—my ears are still ringing. All your work—everyone's work—

THOMAS SINCLAIR: No, no.

LOUISA BARRETT: I'm sorry I didn't believe you. About Susannah Riley, and those drawings, and—

THOMAS SINCLAIR: You were just looking out for Grace. It's what a good mother should do.

(THOMAS SINCLAIR takes LOUISA BARRETT in his arms.)

LOUISA BARRETT: Her godmother.

THOMAS SINCLAIR: Her mother. Aren't you? In a way we're married already, aren't we? Having a child together.

LOUISA BARRETT: Yes.

(THOMAS SINCLAIR and LOUISA BARRETT kiss.)

THOMAS SINCLAIR: Who is Grace's father?

LOUISA BARRETT: You are.

THOMAS SINCLAIR: Don't tease.

LOUISA BARRETT: I'm not teasing.

THOMAS SINCLAIR: Tell me.

LOUISA BARRETT: I can't.

THOMAS SINCLAIR: I have a right to know.

LOUISA BARRETT: I—no one from here, no one you know. A gentleman. But no one you need to concern yourself about. Trust me?

THOMAS SINCLAIR: All right.

(A knock.)

THOMAS SINCLAIR: Come.

(PETER FRONCZYK *enters.*)

LOUISA BARRETT: What—

PETER FRONCZYK: Ma'am. Mr Sinclair.

THOMAS SINCLAIR: Peter.

PETER FRONCZYK: So what happened, sir?

THOMAS SINCLAIR: One generator out of commission, tiles torn up, a lot of dust. Went off without a hitch.

LOUISA BARRETT: You make it sound like you planned it yourself.

THOMAS SINCLAIR: Of course I planned it myself.

PETER FRONCZYK: It went like clockwork, sir. We took the path along the river off the property and split up.

THOMAS SINCLAIR: The boat was waiting for you?

PETER FRONCZYK: Just where you said.

THOMAS SINCLAIR: Good lad. *(Handing him a thick envelope)* Take this, you've earned it. Let me know where you are.

PETER FRONCZYK: Yes, sir.

THOMAS SINCLAIR: Good luck.

(PETER FRONCZYK exits.)

LOUISA BARRETT: And Daniel Henry Bates and his group will be caught and discredited once and for all. People are starting to feel they need electricity, they won't like dangerous radicals blowing up power stations. Is that it?

THOMAS SINCLAIR: Excellent head for business. It was their idea, I just helped them along. Took a tip from the union-busters and had Peter infiltrate their meetings.

LOUISA BARRETT: What will happen to Peter?

THOMAS SINCLAIR: He'll have to disappear, into the West, I suppose.

LOUISA BARRETT: Is that fair? You make Peter a criminal so you can discredit Daniel Henry Bates?

THOMAS SINCLAIR: I made Peter Fronczyk a hero. And I paid him well. He'll be able to get an education now, become an engineer.

LOUISA BARRETT: How have you made him a hero? A hero to your profits?

THOMAS SINCLAIR: Come now. I told you about my plans, that evening you came to see me about Grace. Don't you remember?

LOUISA BARRETT: The night…

THOMAS SINCLAIR: The night Karl Speyer died. I told you I wanted to generate so much electricity I could start giving it away. To bring it to everyone. Don't you remember that?

LOUISA BARRETT: I thought you were talking about the distant future. A dream.

THOMAS SINCLAIR: The future has a way of catching up with us. That's what I'm going to tell President McKinley next week.

LOUISA BARRETT: McKinley?

THOMAS SINCLAIR: Why not? Right to the top! He knows everyone thinks he's just a tool of the businessmen. That can't do much for a president's self-esteem. I'll give him a chance to shock us all with his courage and vision. He probably won't play along. But it's possible. Anything's possible.

(FREDERICK KRAKAUER *walks down the stairs.*)

FREDERICK KRAKAUER: Very clever. Very clever indeed.

THOMAS SINCLAIR: Krakauer! What are you doing here?

FREDERICK KRAKAUER: Somebody bombed the power station. Had to make sure you were all safe.

(LOUISA BARRETT *runs for the stairs.*)

LOUISA BARRETT: Grace!

FREDERICK KRAKAUER: Shh. She's asleep.

LOUISA BARRETT: Let me by!

THOMAS SINCLAIR: Louisa. I'll go.

LOUISA BARRETT: But—

THOMAS SINCLAIR: (*With a glance at* FREDERICK KRAKAUER) Louisa. She's my daughter.

(THOMAS SINCLAIR *exits.*)

LOUISA BARRETT: Mr Krakauer, this is completely unacceptable!

FREDERICK KRAKAUER: Yes it is. All these accidents happening. And here's a man with a beautiful, talented daughter, and a beautiful, intelligent…friend like

yourself, with a reputation to maintain. And such
tender feelings for her goddaughter. And the man will
not see he's put you all on very thin ice.

(THOMAS SINCLAIR *enters.*)

THOMAS SINCLAIR: Grace is all right, she's sleeping—
how did you get in here, Krakauer?

FREDERICK KRAKAUER: Kitchen door. Servants go to
bed, forget to lock the kitchen door. Happens all the
time. Is there any coffee?

THOMAS SINCLAIR: Cook hasn't started her day. And as
we're all fine, you'd best be moving along.

FREDERICK KRAKAUER: Mr Morgan suspected
something like this. Disloyalty. Conflict of interests.
Giving his electricity away? Powerhouse Three will be
ready for the president to flip the switch next week,
even after this explosion. Even after losing two Chief
Engineers. Remarkable. You've done your job. Maybe
it's time for you to go.

THOMAS SINCLAIR: Is it, do you think?

FREDERICK KRAKAUER: Soon. Sooner than people might
think.

THOMAS SINCLAIR: Then I'd best get back to work.

FREDERICK KRAKAUER: Certain investors are prepared
to offer a compromise. Keep everything going. No
changes. No public announcements. No attempts to
influence presidential policy.

THOMAS SINCLAIR: And?

FREDERICK KRAKAUER: Everybody stays like they are.

THOMAS SINCLAIR: If the investors are unhappy, they
can contact me directly.

FREDERICK KRAKAUER: No. This is as direct as they're
going to be.

THOMAS SINCLAIR: Kind of you to drop by and share your views, Mr Krakauer.

LOUISA BARRETT: Please, Tom. Listen to him.

THOMAS SINCLAIR: This doesn't concern you, Louisa.

LOUISA BARRETT: But Grace—

THOMAS SINCLAIR: This isn't about Grace.

LOUISA BARRETT: Please. You can reach a compromise. Something, anything.

FREDERICK KRAKAUER: Wise words. They'll be remembered. Miss Barrett. *(He exits.)*

THOMAS SINCLAIR: I'd better speak to Mrs Sheehan about locking the kitchen door.

LOUISA BARRETT: That's all you can say? He'll destroy you. All of us.

THOMAS SINCLAIR: I don't think so.

LOUISA BARRETT: But he knows about Grace, he—

THOMAS SINCLAIR: He's guessing. It's a bluff. And if it comes to it, I've got a few things I could threaten to tell the newspapers.

LOUISA BARRETT: Such as?

(The telephone rings, off.)

THOMAS SINCLAIR: Speaking of the newspapers…

(THOMAS SINCLAIR exits. LOUISA BARRETT remains.)

Scene 9:
Market Arcade

(FRANKLIN FISKE enters.)

FRANKLIN FISKE: I've just had a curious meal. Luncheon with Thomas Sinclair.

LOUISA BARRETT: Really?

FRANKLIN FISKE: You had no idea?

LOUISA BARRETT: None at all.

FRANKLIN FISKE: He knows everything about me. And you're the only one I've told.

LOUISA BARRETT: I know how to keep a secret, Franklin.

FRANKLIN FISKE: I'll say. Look, Sinclair told me his plans. Giving electricity away, making an ally of McKinley—have you heard about this?

LOUISA BARRETT: Some of it.

FRANKLIN FISKE: It was very grand. Paying me compliments, offering some sort of mutual protection. I felt I was being wooed in some way. Odd sensation.

LOUISA BARRETT: Isn't it. Why did you ask me here today? People are going to talk about us.

FRANKLIN FISKE: That's the idea. Do you believe Sinclair? I don't necessarily believe him.

LOUISA BARRETT: Do you believe anything?

FRANKLIN FISKE: I believe Sinclair is playing a game for very high stakes.

LOUISA BARRETT: Are you going to publish what he told you?

FRANKLIN FISKE: I can't. Until I find out what happened to Speyer and Fitzhugh, I don't buy Tom Sinclair. And now this power station bombing, it feels too neat. But I can't put my finger on anything. Any thoughts on that?

LOUISA BARRETT: No.

FRANKLIN FISKE: Something else I believe. Sinclair is using me. I'm his insurance policy. He can say that he's told me the whole story and I'll the world, if he isn't around to tell it himself. Trouble is, until I can publish, I'm not making life any safer for Sinclair, and he's made it dangerous for me. Me and anybody else who's seen with him.

LOUISA BARRETT: Anybody?

FRANKLIN FISKE: Anybody close to him, sure.

LOUISA BARRETT: His daughter, too?

FRANKLIN FISKE: I wouldn't put anything past these people. You're in the same kind of danger. You do know that?

LOUISA BARRETT: Yes.

FRANKLIN FISKE: If Sinclair does what he says, he won't live out the year.

LOUISA BARRETT: Then why don't you help him!

FRANKLIN FISKE: I'm helping him whether I like it or not. Maybe you like being put in that position, I don't.

LOUISA BARRETT: What can I do, Franklin?

FRANKLIN FISKE: Well. Here's a thought. You need to do something to put yourself at a safe remove from Sinclair. Eliminate all this unhealthy speculation about how close you are to him.

LOUISA BARRETT: And how do you propose I do that?

FRANKLIN FISKE: Well. I don't suppose you'd consider marrying me?

LOUISA BARRETT: Franklin.

FRANKLIN FISKE: I didn't think so. Consider it anyway. I do love you, by the way. Think it over.

LOUISA BARRETT: I'm so very flattered—

FRANKLIN FISKE: Louisa. You have to do something.

LOUISA BARRETT: Well. I had better try and get some insurance of my own.

(FRANKLIN FISKE *exits.* LOUISA BARRETT *remains.*)

Scene 10:
A river in the Berkshires

GROVER CLEVELAND: *(Singing quietly, off)*
There's a wart on the frog on the bump on the log in
the hole at the bottom of the sea…

(GROVER CLEVELAND enters, much aged, fly fishing.)

GROVER CLEVELAND: *(Singing quietly)*
There's a wart on the frog on the bump on the log in
the hole at the bottom of the sea…

(LOUISA BARRETT watches for a moment.)

GROVER CLEVELAND: *(Singing quietly)*
There's a hole, there's a hole…
(Quietly) Good morning, miss. Don't scare the fish.

LOUISA BARRETT: Mr President? I'm Louisa Barrett.
Headmistress of the Macaulay School in Buffalo.

GROVER CLEVELAND: You're a long way from home.

LOUISA BARRETT: I grew up in the Berkshires. The
newspaper said you were on vacation here at
Tyringham, and I took the train. I was a girl here.

GROVER CLEVELAND: Louisa Barrett? Do I know you?

LOUISA BARRETT: We met in Buffalo, ten years ago now.
I was a teacher then.

GROVER CLEVELAND: Ah, yes. We met at one of the
receptions?

LOUISA BARRETT: At 184 Delaware Avenue.

GROVER CLEVELAND: How is my friend Dexter
Rumsey? Prosperous as ever?

LOUISA BARRETT: Even more so. In addition to meeting
at the reception, we also met afterward, at…the
Iroquois Hotel.

GROVER CLEVELAND: Did we?

LOUISA BARRETT: Yes, sir.

GROVER CLEVELAND: Ah. Have you come for a repeat performance? Come out like a water sprite to trap me and seduce me away from home?

LOUISA BARRETT: I'm hardly laying a trap, sir. Mrs Cleveland told me I might find you here.

GROVER CLEVELAND: You went to the house? You spoke to my wife?

LOUISA BARRETT: Why, yes. Of course.

GROVER CLEVELAND: A woman such as yourself? How dare you set foot in my home—show yourself to a virtuous woman?

LOUISA BARRETT: Well, sir, please remember that I am headmistress of a school, I am not… If you can present yourself to your wife, then surely I can as well.

GROVER CLEVELAND: I hardly think—

LOUISA BARRETT: I came to you all-unknowing. Completely naïve, as I was raised to be. What I remember best is you, sir, threatening the innocent girl who was my former self.

GROVER CLEVELAND: An Educator.

LOUISA BARRETT: Yes.

GROVER CLEVELAND: I remember. Rumsey said, keep listening, she'll be worth the trouble.

LOUISA BARRETT: What?

GROVER CLEVELAND: Surprise, coming from old Rumsey. But I seem to recall he was right.

LOUISA BARRETT: He wasn't. Somebody wasn't.

GROVER CLEVELAND: Suit yourself.

LOUISA BARRETT: I have an appeal to make. For my daughter. Our daughter.

GROVER CLEVELAND: A woman like yourself cannot prove that your child is my daughter. A woman like yourself cannot know such a thing.

LOUISA BARRETT: A woman like myself can know such a thing, though I understand your reasons for hoping not.

GROVER CLEVELAND: If you want money, I don't have any. Even if I did, I wouldn't give it to you. I'm far beyond blackmail now. Mrs Cleveland is the only one who concerns me, and she'll believe me over you. The newspapers won't care anymore.

LOUISA BARRETT: I don't need money. Our daughter was adopted into a fine family, she has no need of money.

GROVER CLEVELAND: What, then?

LOUISA BARRETT: Some facts have come to me. About the power station at Niagara.

GROVER CLEVELAND: Yes, I've followed the work there. I've been reading about the bombing in the papers. The police think it was the nature lovers now. I had assumed it was the unionists.

LOUISA BARRETT: The family which adopted our daughter has an interest in the power station.

GROVER CLEVELAND: And?

LOUISA BARRETT: There is a tension between the investors and the management about how the electricity should be used. Threats have been made. Threats even against your daughter.

GROVER CLEVELAND: I find that hard to believe. Not the threats—that's business as usual. But against a child?

LOUISA BARRETT: It's true. There have been two murders already.

GROVER CLEVELAND: Who is making these threats against a little girl?

LOUISA BARRETT: People acting on behalf of J.P. Morgan and other men known to you.

GROVER CLEVELAND: Deep waters there, miss. Deep waters.

LOUISA BARRETT: They are beholden to you. Perhaps a discreet word—

GROVER CLEVELAND: I could do nothing against the forces involved in building that power station. Even when I was President of the United States. And now that I'm out… My dear, don't trouble your head with power stations. Leave such issues to the men who understand them.

LOUISA BARRETT: Mr President. If you had stood up… You could have been a hero. You were nothing.

GROVER CLEVELAND: Good day to you, Miss. (*He exits.*)

LOUISA BARRETT: You're nothing.

(LOUISA BARRETT *remains. The lights change.*)

Scene 11:
State hospital

(FRANCESCA COATSWORTH *enters, followed by an* ATTENDANT.)

FRANCESCA COATSWORTH: Louisa. Thank God. It's Susannah—they've arrested her for the bombing, they're all under arrest, Daniel Henry Bates—they had her in jail, the common jail downtown, an artist, a teacher, they—

LOUISA BARRETT: What can I do, Francesca?

FRANCESCA COATSWORTH: I didn't know where to turn, you were gone—where did you go, Louisa?

LOUISA BARRETT: I just got back, I found your message, I thought—

FRANCESCA COATSWORTH: Dexter Rumsey said she didn't belong in jail, any woman who could do such a thing must be deranged, hysterical. So he had people come from the State Hospital and bring her here. I gave them a big donation to get her these rooms. Do you think if I spread enough money around, they'll decide she's too ill to stand trial, and release her into my custody? I'll take her away from the city.

LOUISA BARRETT: Francesca. What can I do?

FRANCESCA COATSWORTH: Susannah asked me to write to you. She said she needed to see you. Do you know why? Can you tell me?

LOUISA BARRETT: I don't know, Francesca.

FRANCESCA COATSWORTH: I'll tell her you're here.

(SUSANNAH RILEY *enters, with another* ATTENDANT *guarding her.*)

SUSANNAH RILEY: It's all right, Frannie. Thank you for coming, Miss Barrett.

LOUISA BARRETT: Why did you want to see me?

(SUSANNAH RILEY *looks at* FRANCESCA COATSWORTH.)

FRANCESCA COATSWORTH: Well. Why don't I...

SUSANNAH RILEY: Thank you, Frannie. It's better.

(FRANCESCA COATSWORTH *exits. The* ATTENDANTS *retire to a discreet but watchful distance.*)

SUSANNAH RILEY: We were set up—did you know? That man, Peter Fronczyk. We were so innocent. Whenever we had doubts, he pushed us on. And now he's the only one who hasn't been arrested.

LOUISA BARRETT: Why did you want to see me?

SUSANNAH RILEY: Those drawings. I did them, not Grace Sinclair.

LOUISA BARRETT: Thank you for telling me.

SUSANNAH RILEY: I realized afterward…I'd never want to hurt Grace, whatever her father…I also wanted to say, I wanted to ask you…I'm worried about Grace. She's—

LOUISA BARRETT: I'll look after Grace. I always have.

SUSANNAH RILEY: Thank you. Do you think they'll kill me?

LOUISA BARRETT: Why would they do that?

(Beat)

SUSANNAH RILEY: No one ever thought it could be me. Not even you. It was as if I didn't exist.

LOUISA BARRETT: Pardon?

SUSANNAH RILEY: I went right up to him—a complete stranger!

LOUISA BARRETT: Who did you go up to?

SUSANNAH RILEY: The engineer. Karl Speyer.

LOUISA BARRETT: What did you say to Karl Speyer?

SUSANNAH RILEY: I just went up and introduced myself. In the lobby of the Iroquois Hotel. I said I admired what he was doing. He took me to lunch. Afterward—he was married, with two children—he asked me to go upstairs with him. I said no, I mean, I'd have to be an idiot. But I told him, maybe if we got to know each other better…I asked him to take me for a walk in the moonlight. He met me at the lake. I said I wanted to walk across the part they'd cleared for ice-skating. It was a beautiful night, romantic as anything. He followed me. I kept going further and further. He stopped, he called, it wasn't safe. When I was halfway across, I said oh! Pretending to discover where I was. Oh! Acting frightened. I wasn't frightened. Nature protected me. I said, I'm scared, I can't move, what'll I do? He came to my rescue. And that—that broke the ice between us! His coat pulled him down. I watched him...till he was just...part of the landscape. And then it was like I heard voices, a million birds singing, victory, victory, victory.

LOUISA BARRETT: But his death didn't stop the power station.

SUSANNAH RILEY: No. They put in a replacement.

LOUISA BARRETT: James Fitzhugh.

SUSANNAH RILEY: He was easier. He took walks. That place where the current sweeps the shore. I took you there, remember?

LOUISA BARRETT: And Grace, you took Grace.

SUSANNAH RILEY: Grace didn't see anything—I made sure of that. Will they put me on trial?

LOUISA BARRETT: They've invited you into their homes. It would be a terrible scandal. No, they'd never bother with a trial.

SUSANNAH RILEY: They *will* kill me. Tell them not to kill me! Tell them!

LOUISA BARRETT: Why have you told me all this?

SUSANNAH RILEY: I had a partner in what I did. You might be surprised to learn who my partner was. I knew every secret about the power station, because of my partner. When they come to kill me, I'll tell them who my partner was and— (*Snapping her fingers*) they'll get the same as me. You wouldn't like that.

(SUSANNAH RILEY *exits.* LOUISA BARRETT *remains, and in comes:*)

Scene 12:
Pan-American Exposition

(A MAN *enters, a handkerchief wrapped around something vaguely triangular in his hand. As he passes* LOUISA BARRETT, *he pauses for a moment, then exits purposefully.* MARY TALBERT *enters.)*

MARY TALBERT: Miss Barrett.

LOUISA BARRETT: Mrs Talbert! I'm surprised to see you here with the pleasure-seekers.

MARY TALBERT: Hardly pleasure. I and the other ladies of the National Colored Women's Clubs are trying to let the pleasure-seekers know that, in addition to the display of happy plantation life here at the Exposition, we have arranged to exhibit the achievements of our people.

LOUISA BARRETT: It never stops, does it?

MARY TALBERT: No. It never stops. Have you considered what I've said?

*(*MARIA LOVE *enters.)*

LOUISA BARRETT: Yes, I have. Miss Love!

MARIA LOVE: Ah. Miss Barrett. Mrs Talbert.

MARY TALBERT: Miss Love.

MARIA LOVE: I didn't know you two knew each other.

LOUISA BARRETT: Oh yes, we know each other. In fact, Miss Love, Mrs Talbert and I have been talking, about a plan, for the school, which, well, we can't possibly get any further without you.

MARIA LOVE: Well. Does Mr Rumsey know?

LOUISA BARRETT: Well…

MARY TALBERT: No. We wanted to discuss it with you first. Didn't we, Miss Barrett?

LOUISA BARRETT: Absolutely, Mrs Talbert.

(DEXTER RUMSEY *enters, keeping a low profile.*)

MARIA LOVE: Good, good. We'll just keep it to ourselves for now.

LOUISA BARRETT: A question for another day.

MARIA LOVE: Mr Rumsey!

DEXTER RUMSEY: Ladies. Don't tell on me. I ought to have stationed myself somewhat closer to the receiving line. This is much more Milburn's sort of thing than mine. Have you met President McKinley?

LOUISA BARRETT: Not yet. He seems to be a very friendly man.

DEXTER RUMSEY: He is a relentlessly friendly man. It is a standard of friendliness one cannot possibly hope to match.

(WILLIAM MCKINLEY *enters, massaging his right hand with his left, accompanied by the rest of the usual Buffalo presidential entourage:* JOHN MILBURN, RICHARD WATSON GILDER, *and* JOHN J ALBRIGHT.)

JOHN MILBURN: Marvelous, Mr President. Just marvelous.

WILLIAM MCKINLEY: Let me just get some feeling back into the hand, and I'll get right back to it.

JOHN MILBURN: Of course. Don't want to disappoint the public.

WILLIAM MCKINLEY: How was I doing?

RICHARD WATSON GILDER: Once you hit your stride, sir, you achieved an average of forty-five handshakes per minute.

JOHN MILBURN: What a coup! This is really bringing in the people, sir!

(THOMAS SINCLAIR *enters. The entourage quietly closes ranks around* WILLIAM MCKINLEY.)

THOMAS SINCLAIR: Mr President.

JOHN MILBURN: Ah.

(Beat)

THOMAS SINCLAIR: Thomas Sinclair, Mr President, head of the Niagara—

WILLIAM MCKINLEY: The power station, of course. Mr Roosevelt spoke very highly. I'm due out your way tomorrow, isn't that right?

RICHARD WATSON GILDER: That's right, sir.

THOMAS SINCLAIR: It's going to be a big day for us, sir. If I may—

JOHN MILBURN: Everything ready after that explosion, Sinclair?

WILLIAM MCKINLEY: Say, that's right.

THOMAS SINCLAIR: Everything's on schedule. Sir, if I could—

JOHN J ALBRIGHT: And they've arrested those responsible, so no danger there.

WILLIAM MCKINLEY: Fine work all around. Everybody else has been doing his job, I'd better go do mine.

THOMAS SINCLAIR: Mr President—

WILLIAM MCKINLEY: Pleased to meet you, Mr Sinclair, and I look forward to talking tomorrow.

THOMAS SINCLAIR: Sir! One minute of your time now will make tomorrow very much more worth your while.

JOHN MILBURN: Sinclair, we are on a schedule—

RICHARD WATSON GILDER: Hundreds of voters in line—

JOHN J ALBRIGHT: Tom. You're going too far, now, son.

(Beat)

THOMAS SINCLAIR: Tomorrow, then. Tomorrow.

(WILLIAM MCKINLEY glances quizzically at THOMAS SINCLAIR, and the entourage leads him away. LOUISA BARRETT, THOMAS SINCLAIR, and DEXTER RUMSEY are alone together for the first time. Beat)

DEXTER RUMSEY: Mr Sinclair.

THOMAS SINCLAIR: Mr Rumsey.

DEXTER RUMSEY: Do you know, I believe that it is months since we have spoken.

THOMAS SINCLAIR: I believe you're right. Busy time.

DEXTER RUMSEY: Very busy time for us all.

THOMAS SINCLAIR: Speaking of which, if you'll excuse me.

LOUISA BARRETT: For God's sake. Tom. Mr Rumsey. For God's sake.

THOMAS SINCLAIR: Louisa.

DEXTER RUMSEY: Miss Barrett.

LOUISA BARRETT: You have to speak to each other. You have to. Before it's too late. Before something terrible happens.

DEXTER RUMSEY: Miss Barrett is right as always.

THOMAS SINCLAIR: Shall we say, tomorrow evening?

DEXTER RUMSEY: No. This evening, if you don't mind.

THOMAS SINCLAIR: Where?

LOUISA BARRETT: At my house.

DEXTER RUMSEY: Neutral ground. Fair enough.

THOMAS SINCLAIR: I'll be there.

(A gunshot. Screams. Cries of "The president! The president!" People come running out of the pavilion in panic. DEXTER RUMSEY *turns to see. He walks slowly toward the pavilion, breasting the tide.)*

*(*LOUISA BARRETT *and* THOMAS SINCLAIR *remain. The lights change.)*

Scene 13:
Louisa Barrett's

LOUISA BARRETT: Oh, Tom, I'm so sorry. McKinley—I saw you—you were so close.

THOMAS SINCLAIR: Yes.

LOUISA BARRETT: You may still have a chance…if he recovers…

THOMAS SINCLAIR: If he'd had a chance to announce the idea now, while he put Powerhouse Three on line, he would have been riding a path to glory. I doubt he'll be in that frame of mind again. I'll have to go ahead with the plan on my own, oh, but setting up the lines, increasing our output, it's a massive project, I'm not sure I can manage without federal support.

LOUISA BARRETT: What if he dies? Would Mr Roosevelt…

THOMAS SINCLAIR: Perhaps. Where is Rumsey?

LOUISA BARRETT: He'll come.

THOMAS SINCLAIR: Why are you doing this?

LOUISA BARRETT: Isn't it strange that Rumsey and Albright think of me as the best channel to you? Why do you think that is?

THOMAS SINCLAIR: I don't know. Do you?

LOUISA BARRETT: God I'm afraid I do.

(DEXTER RUMSEY *enters.)*

DEXTER RUMSEY: In all my years, I have never had a day like this.

LOUISA BARRETT: Sit down, Mr Rumsey. Has there been any word about the president's condition?

DEXTER RUMSEY: Thank you, child. No, no news. Mr Sinclair. I am very glad to see you this evening.

THOMAS SINCLAIR: Mr Rumsey.

DEXTER RUMSEY: I am relieved to see you. Afraid I wouldn't find you here.

THOMAS SINCLAIR: I did say I would be here, why were you afraid I wouldn't be?

DEXTER RUMSEY: Because, young man, I feared that, despite my best efforts, you'd have been killed by now. That was a very foolish thing you did today. Very foolish. I have negotiated a temporary stay of execution, if I may be so blunt, but only if I am able to persuade you to give up this ridiculous scheme. Now, tonight.

LOUISA BARRETT: Mr Rumsey—

THOMAS SINCLAIR: He's bluffing.

DEXTER RUMSEY: Do I look as if I am bluffing?

THOMAS SINCLAIR: Nobody worth his salt looks like he's bluffing, now does he?

LOUISA BARRETT: My God.

DEXTER RUMSEY: You speak to me about bluffing. I do not understand what you think you have. What do you have? What leverage do you have for this Robin Hood's dream of giving our corporation's product away? Popular sentiment, as embodied by President William McKinley? I think not. What then?

THOMAS SINCLAIR: Me to know.

LOUISA BARRETT: My God. You both love this, don't you. You don't care about the danger, you don't care what happens to Grace.

DEXTER RUMSEY: What do you mean, Louisa?

LOUISA BARRETT: Grace, my goddaughter, Mr Sinclair's daughter.

DEXTER RUMSEY: Yes. She's a close friend of my daughter Ruth.

LOUISA BARRETT: There have been threats. Against Grace. Mr Krakauer said he would hurt her, and me, if Mr Sinclair didn't do—I mean, if Mr Sinclair did do—Mr Krakauer said—

DEXTER RUMSEY: I know of no threats to Grace, or to you. And I know everything, or so I am told.

LOUISA BARRETT: Mr Krakauer entered Grace's home—Tom, tell him! —trespassed in the middle of the night. And he seems to know things about Grace that—

THOMAS SINCLAIR: Louisa—

LOUISA BARRETT: Tom. Somebody has to stop this. Mr Rumsey, state water inspectors have been bribed. If the public were to learn of this—

DEXTER RUMSEY: Oh, please. Everyone has heard about these alleged bribes. No one has ever proven that there've been bribes. I've never seen any proof of bribes.

LOUISA BARRETT: I have. And so has Daniel Henry Bates. He was telling the truth. He knows everything you've done, Tom. Everything.

THOMAS SINCLAIR: How?

LOUISA BARRETT: I hadn't been able to put it all together until today. I went to see Susannah Riley.

DEXTER RUMSEY: The woman's delusional—

LOUISA BARRETT: She told me she had a partner in everything she did. A partner who'd passed her all the information.

THOMAS SINCLAIR: That's impossible, Bates is lying.

LOUISA BARRETT: No, she had a partner. It was Grace. *(Beat)* I found some of your papers in Grace's art portfolio, weeks ago. "Inspection," they said. With columns of initials, and dates, and dollars. I didn't understand it then. But you'd said she'd been working in your office at home. I think she borrowed papers from your desk. She hid them with her drawings and Susannah could read them during their lesson and copy them. And Grace could return the papers before you got home from work.

THOMAS SINCLAIR: Why? Why would she do that? Why?

LOUISA BARRETT: The night Karl Speyer died, Grace told me: "The only thing my parents ever fought about was electricity."

THOMAS SINCLAIR: Oh God.

LOUISA BARRETT: She was only trying to do what she thought Margaret wanted. She was trying to save the Falls.

DEXTER RUMSEY: So the nature fanatics have proof of some wrongdoing. But Mr Sinclair has very cleverly helped the nature fanatics take themselves out of the picture. The public will not listen to them now.

LOUISA BARRETT: The public will listen to the New York *World*. The *World* has a reporter investigating this. The proof I have will complete his investigation. Unless you two stop putting Grace in danger.

(Beat)

THOMAS SINCLAIR: Remarkable head for business.

DEXTER RUMSEY: Well, of course. I've been training her for years.

LOUISA BARRETT: You have been like a father to me, Mr Rumsey. Tom, you have asked to be my husband. There are no men alive who mean more to me. But look what you're doing. You have set forces in motion you cannot control. Grace could die. I haven't known what to do or where to turn. I even went to…Grace's father, to ask him—

THOMAS SINCLAIR: You—

LOUISA BARRETT: Yes—

THOMAS SINCLAIR: Who is he?

DEXTER RUMSEY: Yes, I know. He's been in touch. Did he remember you?

(Beat)

LOUISA BARRETT: Not at first. Which is understandable. He had been given quite a false idea about me.

DEXTER RUMSEY: Had he?

LOUISA BARRETT: By you.

THOMAS SINCLAIR: You make it sound like he already knows all about it.

LOUISA BARRETT: Of course he knows all about it. He planned it.

THOMAS SINCLAIR: Planned what?

DEXTER RUMSEY: Not the child. We didn't expect the child.

LOUISA BARRETT: You gave him the idea that I was… that kind of woman. And that was how he used me.

DEXTER RUMSEY: Don't judge us harshly, my dear. We needed to do what was best. For the city.

LOUISA BARRETT: For the city?

DEXTER RUMSEY: We knew he'd be looking for someone. That was his nature, always, to want someone—

THOMAS SINCLAIR: Who is he? Who is the father of my child?

DEXTER RUMSEY: —I find it hard to understand a man so ruled by pleasure that he would risk everything for it. But, we must deal with the world as we find it, not as we wish it would be.

LOUISA BARRETT: Go on.

DEXTER RUMSEY: Why not guide him, we thought. To someone we could trust. So he wouldn't embarrass himself—and us—with another indiscretion like that Halpin woman. It nearly cost him the White House the first time.

THOMAS SINCLAIR: Holy Sweet Mother of God.

DEXTER RUMSEY: We couldn't let it happen again, not here. You seemed perfect in every way. We knew you were trustworthy. You seemed to understand.

LOUISA BARRETT: I knew nothing. I was innocent.

DEXTER RUMSEY: Now there you surprise me. I remember that night very clearly. I watched you seduce him. With flattery, deference, attention. You made yourself available to be alone with him. You did it all.

LOUISA BARRETT: Mr Rumsey, it was a kind of rape. Don't believe him, Tom, please don't.

DEXTER RUMSEY: Buffalo has been very good to you. Haven't you been happy with how we've treated you all these years?

LOUISA BARRETT: Who is "we"?

DEXTER RUMSEY: A few of us—what does it matter? Albright, Milburn. We were afraid you might leave

Buffalo with your infant to make a new life under a new name. We wanted to keep a watchful eye on you. So we offered you some inducements to stay. We made you headmistress of the Macaulay School. You've never suffered, Louisa, have you?

LOUISA BARRETT: I bore a child.

DEXTER RUMSEY: I am the only one who knows that for certain. But. We must agree to a compromise. I must insist, Mr Sinclair, that you give up your plans to play Robin Hood.

THOMAS SINCLAIR: And how do you propose to stop me?

DEXTER RUMSEY: Through Miss Barrett of course.

LOUISA BARRETT: Pardon?

DEXTER RUMSEY: If he doesn't give up his plans, secrets we would all prefer to keep will become common knowledge.

THOMAS SINCLAIR: I see.

DEXTER RUMSEY: I believe you are a gentleman after all. Despite your background and whatnot. Well?

LOUISA BARRETT: Tom. Don't give in to this.

DEXTER RUMSEY: What would you say to a move to the West?

LOUISA BARRETT: No!

DEXTER RUMSEY: A new project. A dam in a canyon of the Salt River, in Arizona. For electricity and irrigation. A tremendous opportunity, a tremendous challenge.

THOMAS SINCLAIR: I'm surprised you're offering it to me, Mr Rumsey.

DEXTER RUMSEY: Mr Sinclair. Your true leverage has always been your own rare talents. You can write your own ticket. But you cannot expect to write a lot of other people's as well.

LOUISA BARRETT: Tom. What about Grace?

THOMAS SINCLAIR: I'd have to take her with me.

LOUISA BARRETT: No, Tom.

DEXTER RUMSEY: She could live here with my daughter Ruth, if you wish.

LOUISA BARRETT: If Grace stays in Buffalo she should stay with me. I am her mother. I am Grace's mother.

(Beat)

THOMAS SINCLAIR: Grace has to come with me, Louisa.

LOUISA BARRETT: Why?

THOMAS SINCLAIR: If she stays here, she'll be a hostage. It's the only way to keep her safe.

DEXTER RUMSEY: What an adventure this will be for her.

LOUISA BARRETT: If Grace is leaving, I have to leave with her.

DEXTER RUMSEY: My dear girl, I'm afraid that is impossible. We can't lose you and Grace.

LOUISA BARRETT: Why not?

DEXTER RUMSEY: For the reason Mr Sinclair just stated.

LOUISA BARRETT: A hostage. I'm a hostage.

DEXTER RUMSEY: That is far too strong an expression.

LOUISA BARRETT: Tom, you go ahead with what you've been planning. I'll take Grace somewhere. We'll change our names. If Peter could do it, so can I.

THOMAS SINCLAIR: Louisa. If you lose your place in society, Grace loses hers as well. We don't want that kind of life for her. No one will chase after Peter, he's not important—not like you and Grace. They'll find you and use you again.

LOUISA BARRETT: But—

THOMAS SINCLAIR: Our only chance is to fight another day. How old is he, anyway?

LOUISA BARRETT: Tom.

DEXTER RUMSEY: No, Louisa, listen to him.

THOMAS SINCLAIR: Who's going to replace him when he goes? If we hold steady and plot as they plot, we'll win in the end.

DEXTER RUMSEY: So we're agreed then.

THOMAS SINCLAIR: When do we go?

DEXTER RUMSEY: A few weeks should suffice, shouldn't it?

LOUISA BARRETT: God.

THOMAS SINCLAIR: I want my deputies to take over the power station.

DEXTER RUMSEY: You want us to continue your policy with regard to the unions.

THOMAS SINCLAIR: No force.

DEXTER RUMSEY: As long as they use no violence, I will do the same. So, everything is resolved, and so neatly too. We should arrange a hero's farewell for him, shouldn't we, Louisa?

(THOMAS SINCLAIR *exits.*)

LOUISA BARRETT: Mr Rumsey. Is Grace safe now?

DEXTER RUMSEY: Louisa, you are under my protection. You and Grace, both. My deepest protection. As you always have been.

(DEXTER RUMSEY *exits.* LOUISA BARRETT *remains.*)

(*The lights change.*)

(GRACE SINCLAIR *enters.*)

GRACE SINCLAIR: I saw you in my new telescope.

LOUISA BARRETT: I'm glad you like it, sweetheart. I thought you'd be getting ready for your party.

GRACE SINCLAIR: I am ready. We're leaving at one o'clock.

LOUISA BARRETT: Which party is this?

GRACE SINCLAIR: The power station people.

LOUISA BARRETT: You've had so many farewell parties. People will be thinking about you until you come back. Think of all you'll see on the train! You'll cross the Mississippi River! It's wider and browner than you can imagine.

GRACE SINCLAIR: I know.

LOUISA BARRETT: What is it, sweetheart?

GRACE SINCLAIR: Papa is angry with me.

LOUISA BARRETT: Why?

GRACE SINCLAIR: Have I always been such a bad girl as I am now?

LOUISA BARRETT: You are not a bad girl.

GRACE SINCLAIR: Papa says I'm a bad girl.

LOUISA BARRETT: Why?

GRACE SINCLAIR: Remember those papers? That got in with my drawings?

LOUISA BARRETT: Yes.

GRACE SINCLAIR: I guess he must have figured out I had them.

LOUISA BARRETT: Grace. Did Miss Riley ever ask you to borrow things from his desk? Papers? About water? To help Niagara Falls.

(GRACE SINCLAIR *nods.*)

LOUISA BARRETT: What did your father say?

GRACE SINCLAIR: He was crying.

LOUISA BARRETT: Grace, Miss Riley should never have asked you to betray your family. It was very wrong of her.

GRACE SINCLAIR: So she's bad and Papa's good, and I did the worst thing ever.

LOUISA BARRETT: No, no. I know it's hard to figure all this out.

GRACE SINCLAIR: But Mama wanted to help Niagara Falls too. That's what Mama and Papa were fighting about, and I ran in to make them stop fighting and I surprised Mama and she fell down because I surprised her and then she died. And it's all my fault.

LOUISA BARRETT: (*Holding her*) You're a child. Grace, you can't blame yourself for something someone made you do. You can't. You thought you were doing the right thing. That has to count for something. It has to. Sweetheart. Remember when Miss Riley said how hard it is to paint a picture of Niagara? So many different reflections, so many little pieces of picture in the picture, and each one facing its own way, and the faces change all the time. Only God could see all of it at once. We'll never know enough to do everything right. All we can do is try. And you did try.

GRACE SINCLAIR: I wish my mother was here.

(GRACE SINCLAIR *crosses away from* LOUISA BARRETT. LOUISA BARRETT *sobs. Beat*)

(THOMAS SINCLAIR *enters, deeply shaken.*)

THOMAS SINCLAIR: She was playing a pretending game. All the children were playing. On the rocks. By the cascades. She slipped. I was off with the men. Congratulating them. I made sure their wives were watching her. Their children were there, the workmen's children, their mothers. They told me she was telling the children about her mother. She said her mother was an angel now.

(GRACE SINCLAIR *starts spinning slowly.*)

THOMAS SINCLAIR: That she could spin around and around until she saw her. She spun around and around on the rocks. She slipped. She fell backward into the water. She hit her head. I heard screaming. The mothers. The men and I ran to the bank. I couldn't reach her. Nobody could reach her in time.

(GRACE SINCLAIR *stops spinning. The lights change.* THOMAS SINCLAIR *and* GRACE SINCLAIR *exit.* LOUISA BARRETT *remains.*)

(*Church bells peal. Out of the dark, the others gradually assemble into her salon.*)

JOHN MILBURN: Ruined.

JOHN J ALBRIGHT: No.

JOHN MILBURN: We are ruined.

JOHN J ALBRIGHT: You exaggerate as usual, Milburn. *You* are ruined.

JOHN MILBURN: Did you see what they did to my portrait in the Buffalo Club?

JOHN J ALBRIGHT: Yes. And as a connoisseur I'm of two minds.

FRANCESCA COATSWORTH: What did they do?

JOHN MILBURN: Defaced it.

JOHN J ALBRIGHT: Literally.

FRANCESCA COATSWORTH: People were bitter.

JOHN J ALBRIGHT: And what with one loss of face and another, we saw rather less of you after that year, didn't we?

JOHN MILBURN: Well, I was a pariah, wasn't I. An outcast. Untouchable.

FRANCESCA COATSWORTH: What happened to you?

JOHN MILBURN: I went to New York City and became a corporate lawyer.

FRANCESCA COATSWORTH: And you, Mr Krakauer, you left Buffalo, when—

FREDERICK KRAKAUER: The day after the president was shot. Mr J P Morgan suddenly needed me elsewhere. Part of the job.

JOHN J ALBRIGHT: You vanished without a trace, Krakauer.

FREDERICK KRAKAUER: Absolutely, sir. None of you ever heard the name Frederick Krakauer again. I liked that name, too.

FRANKLIN FISKE: Well, but here we are again.

DEXTER RUMSEY: Yes, what is the occasion for this salon? What is our theme?

LOUISA BARRETT: No occasion.

FREDERICK KRAKAUER: Do you ever hear from Tom Sinclair?

LOUISA BARRETT: Less and less. Stories float around. He went into the West, he builds things there. Did you know a boy named Peter Fronczyk?

FRANKLIN FISKE: We never met.

LOUISA BARRETT: He works as Tom's Chief Engineer.

DEXTER RUMSEY: What happened to the Salt River Project in Arizona?

FRANKLIN FISKE: It was as ambitious as you thought, and more. Needed federal funds to go forward.

DEXTER RUMSEY: You mean…

FRANKLIN FISKE: Yes, the government built a utility. The Theodore Roosevelt Dam.

DEXTER RUMSEY: Dear oh, dear. What happened?

THOMAS SINCLAIR: Well among other things, poor people's houses got light.

DEXTER RUMSEY: And young Franklin Fiske?

FRANKLIN FISKE: Reports for the *World*.

LOUISA BARRETT: That he does. He's everywhere.

FRANKLIN FISKE: But I never could print that power station story. All the country could hear about Buffalo was assassination. Then and for years after.

DEXTER RUMSEY: Dear oh dear.

FRANCESCA COATSWORTH: Ever married?

LOUISA BARRETT: No.

FRANKLIN FISKE: Not yet.

LOUISA BARRETT: Not yet.

FRANCESCA COATSWORTH: Ho ho.

LOUISA BARRETT: Jealous?

FRANCESCA COATSWORTH: Jealous of what? *I* went to Angkor Wat.

LOUISA BARRETT: Good for you, Frannie.

FRANCESCA COATSWORTH: Got Susannah released from the hospital and off we went, female explorers in khaki skirts, riding a line of elephants.

SUSANNAH RILEY: We disappeared in Singapore.

FRANCESCA COATSWORTH: Or so the story goes. Died of an Asian fever.

SUSANNAH RILEY: Or so the story goes.

DEXTER RUMSEY: And I passed on in—what was it, Milburn?

JOHN MILBURN: 1906, Mr Rumsey.

DEXTER RUMSEY: 1906, that's right. Seventy-nine. My Biblical span of three score and ten, plus the dividend a good investment deserves. And Buffalo was changing.

JOHN MILBURN: No one took your place.

FRANCESCA COATSWORTH: No one could.

JOHN J ALBRIGHT: You hadn't groomed anyone.

DEXTER RUMSEY: No one to groom, really.

JOHN J ALBRIGHT: The directorship of the Macaulay School board rotates from year to year.

DEXTER RUMSEY: Must be a terrible vacuum in leadership. Who holds the power?

LOUISA BARRETT: I do. You groomed me.

THOMAS SINCLAIR: I told you. Excellent head for business.

LOUISA BARRETT: I think we attract the brightest and most gifted young women in the city.

MARY TALBERT: In the whole city.

DEXTER RUMSEY: What about Buffalo?

LOUISA BARRETT: Well. There's more fluidity. The leadership is more diverse. As Mary Talbert said:

MARY TALBERT: The great desire of our nation to produce the most perfect form of government, shows incontestable proofs of advance.

DEXTER RUMSEY: I don't think I'd care for it. Anything else?

LOUISA BARRETT: (Aside) Let's not tell him about the Saint Lawrence Seaway.

FRANCESCA COATSWORTH: Maria Love lived on at 184 Delaware Avenue until she died, ninety-one years old, in 1931.

JOHN J ALBRIGHT: Which is when I went, too. Purely coincidence, I assure you.

LOUISA BARRETT: But you, Mr Albright.

THOMAS SINCLAIR: Yes, you, John.

DEXTER RUMSEY: What?

JOHN MILBURN: Gave his money away!

JOHN J ALBRIGHT: Lost some of it.

JOHN MILBURN: Gave his money away!

DEXTER RUMSEY: Why, Albright?

JOHN J ALBRIGHT: Gentlemen, honestly, what a stupid question.

JOHN MILBURN: I'm serious. Why?

JOHN J ALBRIGHT: To quote our Miss Barrett...all we can do is try.

LOUISA BARRETT: And the gallery is still there.

JOHN J ALBRIGHT: Yes it is. Though, Miss Barrett? What is that black thing attached to it?

LOUISA BARRETT: Don't you like it?

JOHN J ALBRIGHT: I haven't made up my mind. It looks like...the Twentieth Century.

FRANKLIN FISKE: President William McKinley is remembered for only one thing, I'm afraid.

FREDERICK KRAKAUER: Getting assassinated.

DEXTER RUMSEY: Dear oh dear.

FREDERICK KRAKAUER: President Grover Cleveland died in 1908, aged seventy-one.

LOUISA BARRETT: He is remembered for only two things. Class?

ALL: The only president who served two non-consecutive terms!

FRANCESCA COATSWORTH: And I don't know the other one.

FRANKLIN FISKE: He is remembered for his remarkable, lifelong integrity. Mark Twain—Mark Twain! —said he was on the same moral plane as George Washington.

FREDERICK KRAKAUER: His dying words were, "I have tried so hard to do right."

FRANKLIN FISKE: Any thoughts on that, Louisa?

LOUISA BARRETT: I think…all we can do is try.

JOHN J ALBRIGHT: And some really ought to try harder.

FRANKLIN FISKE: And then there was President Teddy Roosevelt…

FREDERICK KRAKAUER: Who is just a whole 'nother story.

FRANCESCA COATSWORTH: And you, Louisa?

LOUISA BARRETT: Oh, I've begun to think I'll never die. I thought I would. I thought I would. It would have meant something then. But without all of you…

THOMAS SINCLAIR: We're with you in spirit.

LOUISA BARRETT: Yes you are. But without your friends…

DEXTER RUMSEY: What would you be?

LOUISA BARRETT: That's right. What would you be.

GRACE SINCLAIR: Mama? What about Niagara Falls?

LOUISA BARRETT: Oh, sweetheart. Niagara Falls is still there.

GRACE SINCLAIR: Good.

LOUISA BARRETT: During the day, they divert half
the water to electrical generators. Three-quarters of
the water at night. They say it still looks remarkably
natural.

JOHN J ALBRIGHT: But we all have to grow up
sometime.

LOUISA BARRETT: One time, some work had to be done
by the American Falls. So they turned it off. Like a
tap. And then when they were done they turned it on
again.

JOHN MILBURN: What a coup.

GRACE SINCLAIR: It must have seemed like a miracle.

THOMAS SINCLAIR: Unless you know how it was done.

LOUISA BARRETT: Unless you know how it was done.

(LOUISA BARRETT *reaches for the lamp. It is an electric
lamp. She switches it off.*)

END OF PLAY

www.ingramcontent.com/pod-product-compliance
Lightning Source LLC
Chambersburg PA
CBHW052109090426
42741CB00009B/1739